DEFENSE IN DEPTH

NETWORK SECURITY AND CYBER RESILIENCE

4 BOOKS IN 1

BOOK 1
DEFENSE IN DEPTH DEMYSTIFIED: A BEGINNER'S GUIDE TO NETWORK SECURITY AND CYBER RESILIENCE

BOOK 2
MASTERING DEFENSE IN DEPTH: ADVANCED STRATEGIES FOR NETWORK SECURITY AND CYBER RESILIENCE

BOOK 3
FROM NOVICE TO NINJA: THE COMPREHENSIVE GUIDE TO DEFENSE IN DEPTH IN NETWORK SECURITY

BOOK 4
DEFENSE IN DEPTH MASTERY: EXPERT-LEVEL TECHNIQUES FOR UNPARALLELED CYBER RESILIENCE IN NETWORK SECURITY

ROB BOTWRIGHT

Published by Rob Botwright
Library of Congress Cataloging-in-Publication Data
ISBN 978-1-83938-611-4
Cover design by Rizzo

Disclaimer

The contents of this book are based on extensive research and the best available historical sources. However, the author and publisher make no claims, promises, or guarantees about the accuracy, completeness, or adequacy of the information contained herein. The information in this book is provided on an "as is" basis, and the author and publisher disclaim any and all liability for any errors, omissions, or inaccuracies in the information or for any actions taken in reliance on such information. The opinions and views expressed in this book are those of the author and do not necessarily reflect the official policy or position of any organization or individual mentioned in this book. Any reference to specific people, places, or events is intended only to provide historical context and is not intended to defame or malign any group, individual, or entity. The information in this book is intended for educational and entertainment purposes only. It is not intended to be a substitute for professional advice or judgment. Readers are encouraged to conduct their own research and to seek professional advice where appropriate. Every effort has been made to obtain necessary permissions and acknowledgments for all images and other copyrighted material used in this book. Any errors or omissions in this regard are unintentional, and the author and publisher will correct them in future editions.

BOOK 1 - DEFENSE IN DEPTH DEMYSTIFIED: A BEGINNER'S GUIDE TO NETWORK SECURITY AND CYBER RESILIENCE

BOOK 2 - MASTERING DEFENSE IN DEPTH: ADVANCED STRATEGIES FOR NETWORK SECURITY AND CYBER RESILIENCE

BOOK 3 - FROM NOVICE TO NINJA: THE COMPREHENSIVE GUIDE TO DEFENSE IN DEPTH IN NETWORK SECURITY

BOOK 4 - DEFENSE IN DEPTH MASTERY: EXPERT-LEVEL TECHNIQUES FOR UNPARALLELED CYBER RESILIENCE IN NETWORK SECURITY

Introduction

Welcome to the world of "Defense in Depth: Network Security and Cyber Resilience," an immersive and comprehensive book bundle that takes you on a journey through the intricate and ever-evolving landscape of network security and cyber resilience. In today's digitally connected age, where organizations and individuals rely heavily on technology, safeguarding digital assets and data is paramount. Cyber threats continue to evolve, becoming more sophisticated and relentless, making it essential for individuals and organizations to develop robust defense strategies.

Our book bundle is divided into four distinct volumes, each meticulously crafted to cater to different levels of expertise and to provide a holistic understanding of network security and cyber resilience. Whether you are just beginning your journey into the world of cybersecurity or are a seasoned professional seeking to master advanced techniques, this bundle has something for everyone.

In "Defense in Depth Demystified," we start with a Beginner's Guide to Network Security and Cyber Resilience. Here, we lay the foundation for newcomers to the field, breaking down complex concepts into easily understandable components. This volume serves as a launchpad for those looking to embark on a rewarding journey into the world of cybersecurity.

Moving on to "Mastering Defense in Depth," we delve into Advanced Strategies for Network Security and Cyber Resilience. This volume is designed for individuals who wish to elevate their knowledge and skills to the next level. We explore cutting-edge strategies, technologies, and best practices to help you protect your digital assets from ever-evolving threats.

The third volume, "From Novice to Ninja," is a Comprehensive Guide to Defense in Depth in Network Security. It is a comprehensive toolkit for those seeking a well-rounded understanding of network security. We cover topics ranging from network architecture to advanced threat intelligence and access control, equipping readers with the tools needed to create a strong and resilient security posture.

Finally, in "Defense in Depth Mastery," we unlock Expert-Level Techniques for Unparalleled Cyber Resilience in Network Security. This volume is tailored for experts and cybersecurity professionals looking to master the most advanced and sophisticated cybersecurity techniques. We dive deep into incident response methodologies, encryption strategies, and access control to ensure your organization stands strong against even the most determined cyber threats.

In each volume, we emphasize the importance of a proactive and layered defense strategy. Cybersecurity is not a destination; it's a journey that requires continuous learning and adaptation. Throughout this bundle, you will gain insights into the evolving threat landscape and learn how to adapt and respond effectively to the challenges that lie ahead.

Whether you are a newcomer to the field or an experienced cybersecurity practitioner, "Defense in Depth: Network Security and Cyber Resilience" will empower you with the knowledge, tools, and strategies necessary to protect your digital world. As you embark on this journey, remember that the pursuit of cybersecurity excellence is a commitment to the safety and resilience of your digital assets.

BOOK 1
DEFENSE IN DEPTH DEMYSTIFIED
A BEGINNER'S GUIDE TO NETWORK SECURITY AND CYBER RESILIENCE

ROB BOTWRIGHT

Chapter 1: Understanding the Basics of Network Security

In the ever-evolving landscape of the digital age, network security has become an imperative concern, a critical cornerstone in safeguarding sensitive information and ensuring the uninterrupted operation of systems and services. It is not an exaggeration to say that, today, nearly every facet of our lives relies on the seamless functioning of networks, from our personal communications to the operations of global enterprises, governments, and critical infrastructure. Yet, this very dependence on networks also exposes us to an array of potential threats and vulnerabilities that have grown in sophistication and magnitude, requiring us to delve deep into the world of network security to defend against these relentless adversaries.

Understanding the fundamentals of network security is the first step in this journey. It lays the groundwork for building a strong and resilient defense against an array of cyber threats, both known and emerging. Network security encompasses a broad spectrum of principles, technologies, and best practices designed to protect the confidentiality, integrity, and availability of data and services within a networked environment.

At its core, network security strives to create a secure environment where authorized users can access the resources they need while preventing unauthorized users from gaining access or compromising data integrity. Achieving this balance between accessibility and security is a constant challenge, particularly in an era where cyberattacks are becoming increasingly sophisticated and frequent.

To navigate this complex landscape effectively, it's crucial to comprehend the basic concepts, principles, and components that form the foundation of network security. This knowledge will not only empower you to implement robust security measures but also enable you to adapt to the evolving threat landscape and stay one step ahead of potential attackers.

In this book, we will embark on a comprehensive journey through the essential elements of network security. From understanding the basics of network architecture and common threat vectors to exploring the significance of encryption and access control, we will delve into the intricacies of securing modern networks. Throughout this journey, we will provide you with the knowledge and tools necessary to make informed decisions, design effective security strategies, and implement best practices that will help you defend against a wide range of cyber threats.

As we proceed, you'll discover that network security is not a one-size-fits-all endeavor but rather a multifaceted discipline that requires a tailored approach based on specific needs, risks, and objectives. It encompasses a variety of technologies, including firewalls, intrusion detection and prevention systems, encryption, access control, and more, all of which must work together seamlessly to create a robust security posture.

Moreover, network security is not a static field. It continually evolves as new technologies emerge, new vulnerabilities are discovered, and new threats materialize. Staying current with the latest developments is vital for any network security professional or anyone responsible for the security of their organization's network infrastructure.

In the chapters that follow, we will explore the building blocks of network security, starting with an overview of the fundamental concepts and principles. We will then dive deeper into topics such as threat analysis, network design, access control, and encryption. Each chapter will provide a comprehensive understanding of its respective subject matter, equipping you with the knowledge and skills necessary to enhance the security of your networks and systems.

Whether you are new to the field of network security or seeking to expand your expertise, this book aims to be a valuable resource for you. It is designed to cater to a broad audience, including IT professionals, network administrators, cybersecurity enthusiasts, and anyone interested in safeguarding digital assets.

We encourage you to approach this book with curiosity and a willingness to learn. Network security is a dynamic and exciting field, and by mastering its fundamentals, you will be better prepared to face the challenges and opportunities that the digital world presents. So, without further ado, let's embark on this enlightening journey into the realm of network security and equip ourselves with the essential knowledge and skills needed to protect the interconnected world we rely on.

In the realm of network security, understanding the common threats and vulnerabilities that can compromise the integrity and availability of your systems is of paramount importance. These threats come in various forms, often exploiting weaknesses in network architecture, software, or human behavior. One of the most prevalent threats in today's interconnected world is malware, which encompasses a wide range of malicious software designed to infiltrate, damage, or steal data from a network or device. Malware can take the form of viruses, worms, Trojans, ransomware, spyware, and more, each with its own malicious objectives and methods of propagation.

Phishing attacks are another significant threat, where attackers use deceptive emails, websites, or messages to trick individuals into revealing sensitive information or clicking on malicious links. Social engineering attacks, often leveraged in phishing attempts, manipulate human psychology to gain unauthorized access to systems or obtain confidential information. These attacks prey on trust, curiosity, fear, or a desire to help, making them difficult to defend against solely through technical means.

Vulnerabilities in software and systems are a constant concern, as they provide entry points for attackers to exploit. These vulnerabilities can be the result of coding errors, misconfigurations, or unpatched software. A zero-day vulnerability is particularly perilous, as it is a flaw in software that the vendor is unaware of or has not yet patched, leaving systems vulnerable to exploitation.

Denial of Service (DoS) and Distributed Denial of Service (DDoS) attacks disrupt network services by overwhelming them with a flood of traffic. Attackers may flood a network or server with traffic, causing it to become unavailable to legitimate users, or they may use a botnet to coordinate a large-scale attack.

Another vulnerability often exploited is weak or compromised credentials. When users employ weak passwords or reuse the same passwords across multiple accounts, it becomes easier for attackers to gain unauthorized access through credential stuffing or brute force attacks.

Insufficient access controls and privilege escalation vulnerabilities can allow attackers to gain unauthorized access to systems or escalate their privileges once inside. These vulnerabilities can lead to unauthorized data access, manipulation, or system compromise.

Unencrypted communication channels can expose sensitive data to eavesdropping and interception by attackers. This is particularly concerning when transmitting confidential information over public or untrusted networks.

Insecure or outdated protocols, such as outdated versions of the Secure Sockets Layer (SSL) and Transport Layer Security (TLS) protocols, can expose vulnerabilities that attackers can exploit to intercept or manipulate data in transit.

Human error is a significant factor in security breaches. Users may inadvertently click on malicious links, mishandle sensitive data, or fail to follow security best practices, making them vulnerable to various types of attacks.

Outdated or unpatched software and systems are vulnerable to known exploits and vulnerabilities that attackers can readily exploit. Regularly applying patches and updates is essential to mitigate these risks.

Physical security lapses, such as unauthorized access to server rooms or the theft of physical devices, can compromise network security and lead to data breaches.

Inadequate monitoring and logging can make it challenging to detect and respond to security incidents promptly. Without comprehensive logs and monitoring systems in place, malicious activities may go unnoticed.

In summary, network security requires a multifaceted approach to defend against the myriad of threats and vulnerabilities that exist in today's digital landscape. It involves not only implementing technical safeguards but also educating users, establishing robust policies and procedures, and maintaining vigilant monitoring and response capabilities. By understanding common threats and vulnerabilities, organizations can take proactive steps to enhance their security posture and reduce the risk of compromise.

Chapter 2: Cyber Threat Landscape: What You Need to Know

In the ever-evolving world of cybersecurity, staying informed about the current cyber threat landscape is essential for organizations and individuals alike. Cyber threats are dynamic and continually evolving, driven by technological advancements, changing attack techniques, and the ever-present motivation of cybercriminals. In today's interconnected and digital world, the threat landscape has expanded exponentially, presenting a complex and multifaceted challenge to cybersecurity professionals and organizations.

One of the most significant factors shaping the current threat landscape is the increasing sophistication of cyberattacks. Attackers are continually developing new tactics, techniques, and procedures (TTPs) to bypass security measures and exploit vulnerabilities. These TTPs often leverage advanced malware, evasion techniques, and social engineering tactics, making it increasingly challenging to detect and defend against cyber threats effectively.

Advanced Persistent Threats (APTs) are a notable component of the modern cyber threat landscape. APTs are highly sophisticated and targeted attacks that often originate from well-funded and organized threat actors, such as nation-states or advanced cybercriminal groups. APTs are characterized by their persistence, stealth, and the strategic use of multiple attack vectors over an extended period.

Ransomware attacks have also gained prominence in recent years. These attacks involve encrypting a victim's data and demanding a ransom for its decryption. Ransomware has become more destructive and lucrative for cybercriminals, leading to widespread incidents that can disrupt critical services and cause significant financial losses.

Supply chain attacks have emerged as a significant concern, with attackers targeting software vendors and service providers to compromise the security of their customers indirectly. These attacks can have far-reaching consequences, impacting organizations that rely on the compromised supply chain.

Nation-state-sponsored cyberattacks continue to be a major source of concern, as governments engage in cyber espionage, information warfare, and disruptive activities against other nations, organizations, or critical infrastructure. These attacks can have geopolitical implications and escalate tensions between nations.

The proliferation of Internet of Things (IoT) devices has introduced new attack surfaces and vulnerabilities into the cyber threat landscape. Insecurely configured IoT devices can be easily compromised and used in large-scale botnets for distributed denial-of-service (DDoS) attacks or other malicious activities.

Phishing attacks remain a prevalent threat, with attackers using increasingly convincing social engineering tactics to deceive users into divulging sensitive information, clicking on malicious links, or downloading malware. Spear-phishing, a targeted form of phishing, involves customized attacks against specific individuals or organizations.

Cryptocurrency-related threats have also surged, with attackers using cryptocurrency for ransom payments and conducting cryptojacking operations to mine digital currencies using compromised resources.

The expansion of remote work and the increased use of cloud services have created new challenges in securing distributed and virtualized environments. Attackers have exploited remote access vulnerabilities, misconfigured cloud services, and weak authentication to gain unauthorized access to corporate networks and data.

The Dark Web and underground cybercriminal communities continue to thrive, providing a marketplace for cybercriminals to buy, sell, and exchange tools, services, and stolen data. These hidden forums facilitate the development and dissemination of cyber threats.

Machine learning and artificial intelligence (AI) are being used by both defenders and attackers. While AI-powered security solutions can help detect and respond to threats more effectively, cybercriminals are also using AI to automate attacks, personalize phishing campaigns, and enhance malware evasion techniques.

Cybersecurity professionals face the ongoing challenge of keeping pace with the evolving threat landscape. Threat intelligence, information sharing, and collaboration within the cybersecurity community are vital components of a proactive defense strategy. Organizations must also prioritize cybersecurity awareness and training for their employees to mitigate the human element of cyber risk.

In summary, the current cyber threat landscape is marked by its complexity and dynamism. To defend against the evolving array of cyber threats, organizations and individuals must adopt a proactive and adaptive approach to cybersecurity. This involves staying informed, implementing robust security measures, conducting regular risk assessments, and fostering a culture of security awareness and vigilance. As technology continues to advance, so too will the cyber threat landscape, making it imperative to remain vigilant and prepared for the challenges that lie ahead.

The history of cybersecurity is marked by a series of notable incidents and attacks that have left a significant impact on organizations, individuals, and the digital landscape as a whole. These incidents serve as stark reminders of the ever-present threat that cyberattacks pose in our interconnected world. One of the earliest and most infamous incidents was the Morris Worm, unleashed in 1988 by a Cornell University graduate student, Robert Tappan Morris. The worm spread rapidly across the fledgling internet, causing widespread disruptions and leading to the first federal conviction under the Computer Fraud and Abuse Act.

In the early 2000s, the "ILOVEYOU" worm wreaked havoc worldwide, spreading via email and causing massive financial losses. It underscored the vulnerability of email systems to social engineering attacks and led to increased awareness of the need for email security measures.

The Code Red worm, in 2001, exploited a vulnerability in Microsoft's Internet Information Services (IIS) web server software, infecting hundreds of thousands of servers and defacing websites. It was a wake-up call for the importance of timely software patching and updates.

In 2007, Estonia experienced a massive cyberattack that disrupted government, financial, and media websites. The attack was believed to be politically motivated and demonstrated the potential for nation-states to use cyber means for political purposes.

The Stuxnet worm, discovered in 2010, was a highly sophisticated cyber weapon attributed to nation-states. It targeted industrial control systems (ICS) and specifically aimed to disrupt Iran's nuclear program, highlighting the potential for cyberattacks to target critical infrastructure.

In 2013, Edward Snowden's revelations about government surveillance programs, such as PRISM, sent shockwaves worldwide and ignited debates about privacy and surveillance in the digital age.

The massive data breach at Target in 2013 compromised credit card data for over 40 million customers and exposed vulnerabilities in point-of-sale systems, leading to heightened scrutiny of cybersecurity in the retail industry.

The WannaCry ransomware attack in 2017 spread rapidly across the globe, encrypting data on infected computers and demanding ransom payments in Bitcoin. It exploited a vulnerability in Microsoft's Windows operating system, highlighting the risks of unpatched systems.

The Equifax data breach in 2017 exposed sensitive personal information of over 147 million Americans. It showcased the significance of securing customer data and the dire consequences of a data breach.

The NotPetya ransomware attack in 2017, initially disguised as ransomware, was later attributed to nation-state actors and had the primary goal of causing disruption rather than financial gain. It inflicted substantial damage on organizations worldwide.

The SolarWinds supply chain attack, discovered in late 2020, compromised the software updates of a widely used network management tool, allowing attackers to infiltrate numerous government and corporate networks. It exemplified the risks posed by vulnerabilities in the software supply chain.

The Colonial Pipeline ransomware attack in 2021 disrupted the fuel supply chain on the U.S. East Coast, highlighting the vulnerability of critical infrastructure to cyberattacks.

These notable incidents and attacks represent just a fraction of the cybersecurity challenges faced in recent decades. They underscore the evolving nature of cyber threats and the need for constant vigilance and proactive cybersecurity measures. As technology continues to advance, new threats and attack vectors will emerge, necessitating ongoing efforts to secure our digital infrastructure and data.

In response to these incidents and the growing threat landscape, governments, organizations, and cybersecurity professionals have been working tirelessly to enhance cybersecurity measures. This includes increased investment in threat intelligence, advanced security tools and technologies, employee training and awareness programs, and collaboration across sectors to share threat information and best practices.

Cybersecurity has become an integral part of modern life, and the battle against cyber threats is ongoing. It requires a collective effort from individuals, organizations, and governments to protect the digital world we rely on. By learning from the lessons of past incidents and staying vigilant, we can better defend against the ever-evolving landscape of cyber threats.

Chapter 3: Building a Strong Security Foundation

Establishing security policies and best practices is a fundamental aspect of effective cybersecurity management, providing a structured framework for safeguarding information assets and mitigating risks. These policies serve as a foundation upon which organizations can build a robust security posture, ensuring the confidentiality, integrity, and availability of critical data and systems. A well-crafted security policy defines the organization's approach to security, outlining its goals, strategies, and expectations regarding the protection of information and technology resources.

One of the first steps in establishing security policies is defining the organization's security objectives and priorities. These objectives should align with the organization's overall mission and business goals, ensuring that security efforts support and enhance the core mission of the organization. By setting clear objectives, organizations can establish a framework for decision-making and resource allocation in the realm of cybersecurity.

Risk assessment is a crucial component of security policy development. Organizations must identify and assess the various threats and vulnerabilities that could impact their information assets. This includes evaluating the likelihood and potential impact of different security incidents, such as data breaches, malware infections, or system outages. Risk assessments help organizations prioritize security measures and allocate resources effectively.

Once risks are identified, organizations can develop specific security controls and measures to mitigate those risks. These controls encompass a wide range of technical, administrative, and physical safeguards, such as access controls, encryption, intrusion detection systems, and security awareness training. Security controls should be tailored to address the organization's unique risk profile and operational requirements.

Security policies should clearly articulate the roles and responsibilities of individuals and teams within the organization. This includes defining who is responsible for specific security functions, such as network security, data protection, and incident response. Role-based access control (RBAC) and the principle of least privilege (PoLP) can help ensure that individuals have the appropriate level of access to resources based on their job responsibilities.

User awareness and training are vital components of security policies and best practices. Employees, contractors, and other stakeholders should receive regular training on security awareness, safe computing practices, and the organization's specific security policies and procedures. Training programs should be tailored to the organization's needs and may include simulated phishing exercises to test user readiness.

Password policies are a crucial element of security best practices. Passwords are often the first line of defense against unauthorized access. Organizations should establish strong password requirements, enforce password complexity rules, and implement multi-factor authentication (MFA) where possible. Regular password changes and password storage best practices should also be included in the policy.

Data protection and encryption policies are essential for safeguarding sensitive information. These policies define how sensitive data is classified, stored, transmitted, and disposed of securely. Encryption should be employed to protect data both at rest and in transit, and organizations should have clear guidelines for data retention and disposal to ensure compliance with regulatory requirements.

Regular security assessments and audits should be incorporated into security policies to evaluate the effectiveness of security controls and identify areas for improvement. External assessments by third-party security experts and internal audits can help organizations identify vulnerabilities and weaknesses that may not be apparent during routine operations.

Incident response policies are critical for addressing security incidents effectively when they occur. These policies define the procedures for detecting, reporting, and responding to security incidents, such as data breaches, malware infections, or system compromises. They also outline the roles and responsibilities of incident response teams and provide guidance on communication, containment, and recovery efforts.

Compliance with industry regulations and legal requirements is an integral part of security policies. Organizations should be aware of relevant regulations, such as the General Data Protection Regulation (GDPR), the Health Insurance Portability and Accountability Act (HIPAA), or the Payment Card Industry Data Security Standard (PCI DSS), and establish policies and controls to ensure compliance. Compliance policies should include regular audits and reporting to regulatory authorities when necessary.

Security policies and best practices should be dynamic and adaptable to the evolving threat landscape and the organization's changing needs. Regular reviews and updates are essential to ensure that policies remain relevant and effective. Organizations should also promote a culture of security awareness among employees, fostering a sense of responsibility for protecting the organization's information assets.

In summary, establishing security policies and best practices is a foundational element of effective cybersecurity management. These policies provide a structured framework for addressing risks, defining security controls, and guiding the organization's approach to security. By prioritizing security objectives, assessing risks, implementing controls, and promoting user awareness, organizations can build a strong security posture that safeguards their critical data and systems in an increasingly digital world.

Security training and awareness initiatives play a pivotal role in building a robust cybersecurity culture within organizations, equipping employees with the knowledge and skills necessary to identify, prevent, and respond to security threats effectively. In today's interconnected and digital workplace, where cyberattacks continue to evolve in sophistication and frequency, the human element remains a critical factor in defending against these threats. Security training and awareness efforts are designed to bridge the gap between technical security measures and the behaviors of individuals who interact with technology daily.

A well-structured security training program begins with the assessment of an organization's specific needs and risks. Understanding the organization's unique threat landscape, industry requirements, and regulatory obligations is essential in tailoring the training content to address relevant challenges. This assessment helps in identifying the critical areas where employees require education and guidance.

Security training should cover a wide range of topics, starting with fundamental security principles and best practices. Employees should be educated about the basics of password security, safe browsing habits, recognizing phishing attempts, and the importance of regular software updates and patch management. These foundational concepts form the basis for a strong security posture.

Phishing awareness training is particularly crucial, given the prevalence of phishing attacks in the cybersecurity landscape. Employees should be taught to recognize phishing emails, suspicious links, and potential social engineering tactics that cybercriminals often employ to deceive users into revealing sensitive information or executing malicious actions.

Data protection and privacy awareness are also critical components of security training. Employees should understand their responsibilities in safeguarding sensitive data, both personal and organizational. This includes compliance with data protection regulations and internal data handling policies.

Secure communication practices should be emphasized, including the use of encrypted email and messaging platforms for sensitive information. Additionally, employees should be aware of the risks associated with public Wi-Fi networks and the need for using virtual private networks (VPNs) when accessing corporate resources remotely.

Mobile device security is an integral part of modern security training, as smartphones and tablets are widely used in the workplace. Employees should learn how to secure their mobile devices, including setting strong passwords, enabling biometric authentication, and installing security updates promptly.

Security training should extend to the safe use of social media and the risks associated with sharing personal or sensitive information on public platforms. Understanding the potential consequences of oversharing on social media can help mitigate security risks.

A well-rounded security training program should include practical exercises and simulations to reinforce learning.

Phishing simulations, for example, can test employees' ability to identify phishing emails and respond appropriately. These exercises provide real-world scenarios for employees to apply what they have learned.

Security training should not be limited to specific job roles or departments. All employees, from executives to administrative staff, should receive comprehensive security training, as cyberattacks can target individuals at any level of an organization. A security-aware culture should permeate the entire organization.

Regular and ongoing security training is essential, as the threat landscape evolves, and new attack techniques emerge. Employees should receive refresher training sessions and updates to stay current with the latest security threats and best practices.

In addition to formal training sessions, security awareness initiatives can include a variety of awareness campaigns and communication efforts. These initiatives may involve the distribution of security newsletters, posters, and informative emails to keep employees informed about current threats and security tips.

Security champions or advocates within the organization can play a crucial role in promoting security awareness. These individuals are passionate about cybersecurity and can serve as role models and sources of information for their colleagues.

Recognition and rewards can be used to incentivize security-conscious behavior. Recognizing employees who report security incidents or demonstrate exceptional vigilance in identifying threats can foster a culture of security awareness.

Security awareness initiatives should be accessible and easy to understand, avoiding overly technical jargon and complex terminology. The goal is to empower employees with practical knowledge that they can apply in their daily work and personal lives.

In summary, security training and awareness initiatives are integral components of a comprehensive cybersecurity strategy. They empower employees to become active participants in the defense against cyber threats and contribute to building a strong security culture within organizations. By providing relevant, ongoing education and fostering a security-aware mindset, organizations can significantly enhance their resilience against evolving cyber threats.

Chapter 4: Essential Security Tools and Technologies

An essential aspect of modern cybersecurity is the utilization of a variety of security tools and technologies to protect networks, systems, and data from cyber threats. These tools serve as critical components of an organization's defense-in-depth strategy, offering different capabilities and functionalities to address various security challenges. In this overview, we will explore some of the essential security tools and their roles in safeguarding digital assets.

Firewalls, both hardware and software-based, are foundational security tools that establish a perimeter defense for networks. They control incoming and outgoing network traffic based on a set of predefined security rules, allowing or blocking traffic based on criteria such as source IP, destination IP, and port numbers. Firewalls are effective in preventing unauthorized access and filtering out potentially malicious traffic.

Intrusion Detection Systems (IDS) and Intrusion Prevention Systems (IPS) are essential for monitoring network traffic and identifying suspicious or malicious activities. IDS analyze network traffic patterns and raise alerts when anomalies are detected, while IPS not only detect but also take action to block or mitigate threats in real-time. These tools are crucial for early threat detection and response.

Antivirus and anti-malware software are indispensable in defending against a wide range of malicious software, including viruses, worms, Trojans, spyware, and ransomware. They scan files and systems for known malware signatures and behavior patterns, quarantining or removing threats to prevent infection.

Encryption tools and technologies play a pivotal role in securing data both in transit and at rest. Secure Sockets Layer (SSL) and Transport Layer Security (TLS) protocols are used to encrypt data during transmission, while disk encryption solutions protect data stored on devices and servers. Encryption ensures that even if data is intercepted, it remains unreadable to unauthorized parties.

Virtual Private Networks (VPNs) are employed to establish secure and encrypted communication channels over public or untrusted networks. VPNs provide a level of confidentiality and integrity for data transmitted between remote locations or users and the corporate network, protecting it from eavesdropping or tampering.

Security Information and Event Management (SIEM) systems collect and analyze log data from various sources across an organization's IT infrastructure. SIEM tools correlate and analyze this data to detect security incidents, providing insights into potential threats and vulnerabilities. They are invaluable for incident detection, investigation, and reporting.

Access control and authentication tools are crucial for verifying the identity of users and controlling their access to resources. Multi-factor authentication (MFA) adds an extra layer of security by requiring users to provide multiple forms of verification, such as a password and a one-time code sent to their mobile device.

Vulnerability scanning tools are used to assess and identify weaknesses in systems, applications, and network configurations. They scan for known vulnerabilities and misconfigurations, allowing organizations to prioritize and remediate security issues before they are exploited by attackers.

Patch management tools are essential for keeping software, operating systems, and applications up-to-date with the latest security patches and updates. Regularly applying patches helps mitigate known vulnerabilities and reduce the attack surface.

Web Application Firewalls (WAFs) are specialized firewalls designed to protect web applications from a variety of attacks, including SQL injection, cross-site scripting (XSS), and other web-based threats. They inspect incoming web traffic and filter out malicious requests before they reach the application.

Endpoint security solutions are designed to protect individual devices (endpoints) such as laptops, desktops, and mobile devices. These solutions include antivirus software, host-based firewalls, and device encryption, ensuring that endpoints are secure both on and off the corporate network.

Network monitoring and analysis tools provide visibility into network traffic, allowing organizations to detect anomalies and suspicious activities. They are instrumental in identifying network-based threats and performance issues, facilitating incident response and troubleshooting.

Incident response tools and playbooks are used to orchestrate and automate the response to security incidents. They help organizations streamline incident handling processes, ensuring a swift and coordinated response to mitigate the impact of a security breach.

Data loss prevention (DLP) solutions are vital for preventing unauthorized data leaks or exfiltration. DLP tools monitor data movement and enforce policies to prevent sensitive data from being shared, stored, or transmitted outside authorized channels.

Security awareness and training platforms are essential for educating employees and users about security best practices. These platforms provide training modules, simulated phishing exercises, and awareness campaigns to enhance user knowledge and reduce the risk of social engineering attacks.

Security assessment and penetration testing tools are employed to assess an organization's security posture by simulating real-world attacks. Penetration tests identify vulnerabilities and weaknesses, helping organizations prioritize remediation efforts and improve overall security.

Security orchestration, automation, and response (SOAR) platforms enable organizations to automate and streamline security workflows and incident response processes. They integrate with various security tools and provide orchestration capabilities to enhance efficiency and reduce response times.

Security tools must be selected and implemented based on an organization's specific security requirements, risk profile, and operational needs. An effective security strategy combines multiple tools and technologies to create a layered defense approach, addressing various attack vectors and reducing the likelihood of successful breaches.

In summary, essential security tools and technologies are indispensable for safeguarding digital assets in an increasingly interconnected and threat-prone environment. These tools, when integrated into a comprehensive security strategy, provide organizations with the means to detect, prevent, and respond to cyber threats effectively. Staying current with evolving threats and continuously evaluating and updating security tools is essential to maintain a robust defense against cyber adversaries.

Implementing security technologies effectively is a critical aspect of any organization's cybersecurity strategy, as it directly impacts the ability to protect against evolving cyber threats. The deployment of security technologies must align with an organization's overall security objectives and risk management approach. To achieve this alignment, several key considerations and best practices should be followed.

One of the first steps in implementing security technologies effectively is conducting a thorough assessment of an organization's security needs and vulnerabilities. This assessment should involve evaluating the organization's risk profile, current security posture, and existing security technologies in use. It is essential to identify weaknesses, gaps, and areas that require improvement.

Once the assessment is complete, organizations should define clear security goals and objectives. These goals should be specific, measurable, achievable, relevant, and time-bound (SMART) to ensure they align with the organization's overall mission and business objectives. Defining clear goals provides a roadmap for the implementation process.

A crucial aspect of effective implementation is selecting the right security technologies that align with the identified security goals and objectives. Organizations should evaluate available solutions in the market, considering factors such as features, scalability, ease of management, and cost. The chosen technologies should complement existing security infrastructure and address identified vulnerabilities.

It is essential to consider the scalability and flexibility of security technologies. As organizations grow and evolve, their security needs may change. Implementing technologies that can adapt to these changing requirements ensures long-term effectiveness and minimizes the need for frequent replacements.

Effective implementation also involves creating a detailed project plan that outlines the steps, resources, and timelines required for deploying security technologies. A well-defined project plan helps organizations manage the implementation process efficiently and mitigate potential challenges or delays.

Organizations should consider the integration of security technologies with existing systems and processes. Compatibility and interoperability with other security tools and IT infrastructure are crucial for a seamless and efficient security ecosystem. Integration ensures that security technologies work together cohesively to provide comprehensive protection.

User training and awareness are essential components of effective implementation. Employees and users should be educated about the new security technologies, their roles in the organization's security posture, and how to use them correctly. Training programs and resources should be tailored to the needs of different user groups.

Implementation should also involve thorough testing and validation of security technologies before they are deployed in a production environment. This testing phase allows organizations to identify and resolve any issues or configuration errors, ensuring that the technologies function as intended and do not introduce vulnerabilities.

Organizations should establish clear policies and procedures for the use and management of security technologies. These policies should define roles and responsibilities, incident response procedures, and guidelines for configuring and maintaining the technologies. Policies should be regularly reviewed and updated to reflect changes in the threat landscape and technology advancements.

Effective monitoring and continuous improvement are essential components of security technology implementation. Organizations should implement robust monitoring solutions that provide real-time visibility into security events and incidents. This visibility enables rapid detection and response to emerging threats.

Regular audits and assessments of security technologies and practices help organizations identify areas for improvement and ensure compliance with security policies and industry regulations. These assessments should include vulnerability assessments, penetration testing, and security audits.

Collaboration and communication among different teams and stakeholders within the organization are crucial for effective implementation. Security teams, IT teams, and business units should work together to ensure that security technologies align with business objectives and do not hinder productivity.

Vendor relationships and support are essential considerations when implementing security technologies. Organizations should have clear communication channels with vendors, access to timely updates and patches, and a support structure in place to address any issues or concerns that may arise during implementation and operation.

Finally, organizations should regularly evaluate the effectiveness of security technologies through key performance indicators (KPIs) and metrics. These metrics should align with the defined security goals and objectives and provide insights into the technologies' impact on reducing risk and enhancing security posture.

In summary, implementing security technologies effectively requires a strategic and well-structured approach. Organizations must assess their security needs, define clear objectives, select the right technologies, create a detailed implementation plan, and consider scalability, integration, and user training. Regular monitoring, assessment, and collaboration are essential for maintaining the effectiveness of security technologies in an ever-evolving threat landscape. By following best practices and staying proactive, organizations can enhance their cybersecurity defenses and protect their digital assets effectively.

Chapter 5: Securing Your Network Infrastructure

Securing network infrastructure is a paramount concern for organizations in today's digitally connected world, as network environments serve as the backbone of modern business operations and data exchange. A breach in network security can result in significant consequences, including data breaches, service interruptions, and financial losses. To safeguard network infrastructure effectively, organizations must employ a combination of strategies and best practices.

One fundamental strategy for network infrastructure security is the implementation of access controls and authentication mechanisms. Access controls ensure that only authorized users and devices can access network resources, while authentication verifies the identity of users or devices attempting to gain access. Employing strong authentication methods such as multi-factor authentication (MFA) adds an extra layer of security by requiring multiple forms of verification.

Network segmentation is another critical security strategy that involves dividing a network into smaller, isolated segments. Each segment can have its access controls and security policies, reducing the lateral movement of attackers in case of a breach. Network segmentation helps contain potential threats and limit their impact on the overall network.

Firewalls are essential components of network security, acting as gatekeepers that filter incoming and outgoing network traffic. Firewalls enforce security policies by inspecting packets and determining whether they should be allowed or blocked based on predefined rules. Organizations should deploy both perimeter firewalls and internal firewalls to protect different segments of the network.

Intrusion Detection Systems (IDS) and Intrusion Prevention Systems (IPS) play a crucial role in monitoring network traffic for suspicious or malicious activities. IDS analyze network traffic patterns and raise alerts when anomalies are detected, while IPS not only detect but also take action to block or mitigate threats in real-time. These systems provide early threat detection and response capabilities.

Regularly updating and patching network devices and software is a fundamental security practice. Vulnerabilities in network equipment can be exploited by attackers to gain unauthorized access or disrupt network operations. Timely patching and updates help mitigate known vulnerabilities and reduce the attack surface.

Encryption is a critical strategy for protecting data as it travels over the network. Secure Sockets Layer (SSL) and Transport Layer Security (TLS) protocols encrypt data in transit, ensuring that it remains confidential and cannot be intercepted by eavesdroppers. Virtual Private Networks (VPNs) provide encrypted communication channels over public or untrusted networks, safeguarding data during transmission.

Network monitoring and logging are essential for identifying and responding to security incidents. Security Information and Event Management (SIEM) systems collect and analyze log data from various network sources, enabling organizations to detect and investigate security events. Continuous monitoring helps identify abnormal behavior and potential threats in real-time.

Implementing strong password policies is a fundamental security practice. Passwords are often the first line of defense against unauthorized access. Organizations should enforce password complexity requirements, regular password changes, and account lockout policies to prevent brute force attacks.

Network security also encompasses the protection of wireless networks. Organizations should implement strong encryption and authentication mechanisms for Wi-Fi networks, such as WPA3, and regularly review and update wireless security settings to prevent unauthorized access.

Regular security assessments and penetration testing are vital for identifying weaknesses in network infrastructure. Penetration tests simulate real-world attacks to identify vulnerabilities and misconfigurations. These assessments help organizations prioritize remediation efforts and improve overall security.

Implementing robust incident response plans and procedures is crucial for effective network security. Organizations should define clear incident response roles and responsibilities, establish communication protocols, and conduct regular incident response drills to ensure a coordinated and efficient response to security incidents.

Security awareness training for employees is an integral part of network security. Users should be educated about security best practices, including recognizing phishing attempts, safe browsing habits, and the importance of reporting suspicious activities. Training programs should be tailored to the specific security needs of the organization.

Regularly reviewing and updating network security policies and procedures is essential to address evolving threats and compliance requirements. Organizations should also consider industry-specific regulations and standards when defining security policies to ensure compliance.

Implementing network security technologies and strategies is an ongoing process that requires continuous monitoring, assessment, and adaptation to address emerging threats. Collaboration among different teams within the organization, including IT, security, and business units, is essential to align network security efforts with business objectives.

In summary, network infrastructure security is a critical component of overall cybersecurity. Employing strategies such as access controls, network segmentation, firewalls, intrusion detection, and encryption helps organizations protect their network environments from a wide range of threats. Regular updates, monitoring, and employee training are essential elements of an effective network security strategy. By implementing these strategies and staying proactive, organizations can safeguard their network infrastructure in an ever-evolving threat landscape.

Network access control and segmentation are critical components of modern cybersecurity, providing organizations with effective strategies for safeguarding their digital assets and reducing the attack surface. These two complementary approaches enable organizations to control and restrict access to network resources, thereby enhancing security and mitigating risks.

Network access control (NAC) encompasses a range of techniques and technologies designed to regulate and manage the devices and users that connect to a network. NAC solutions enforce security policies, ensuring that only authorized devices and users are granted access while blocking or quarantining unauthorized or non-compliant ones. The goal of NAC is to establish a robust first line of defense against potential threats by controlling who and what can enter the network.

One fundamental aspect of NAC is device identification and authentication. Before allowing a device to access the network, NAC solutions verify its identity and compliance with security policies. This typically involves user authentication, device authentication, and endpoint assessment. Multi-factor authentication (MFA) is often used to enhance security by requiring users to provide multiple forms of verification.

Endpoint security checks are conducted to ensure that devices meet specific security requirements, such as having up-to-date antivirus software, operating system patches, and the latest security updates. Devices that do not meet these requirements may be denied access or placed in a restricted network segment, allowing them to remediate their security posture before full access is granted.

Network access control solutions also play a crucial role in enforcing access policies based on user roles and privileges. Role-based access control (RBAC) allows organizations to define specific access permissions for different user groups or individuals. This ensures that users have access only to the resources necessary for their roles, limiting the risk of unauthorized access to sensitive data.

NAC solutions are effective not only for regulating access to the internal network but also for managing guest and BYOD (Bring Your Own Device) access. Guest access portals can be configured to grant temporary and limited access to visitors, such as clients, contractors, or conference attendees, while segregating them from the internal network.

BYOD policies and NAC can work in tandem to allow employees to use their personal devices while maintaining security. NAC solutions can ensure that BYOD devices meet security standards before granting access, and they can also separate personal and corporate traffic to prevent security risks.

Network segmentation is a complementary strategy that divides a network into smaller, isolated segments or subnetworks. Each segment can have its access controls and security policies, effectively creating barriers that restrict lateral movement in the event of a security breach. The segmentation approach limits the scope of a potential attack and helps contain threats within a specific network segment. Segmentation can be achieved through various methods, including physical separation, virtual LANs (VLANs), and software-defined networking (SDN). Regardless of the method used, the key principle is to isolate different parts of the network to minimize the impact of security incidents.

One common use case for network segmentation is separating critical infrastructure from general corporate traffic. Critical infrastructure, such as industrial control systems (ICS) and supervisory control and data acquisition (SCADA) systems, requires strict isolation to protect against cyberattacks that could disrupt essential operations.

Segmentation is also employed to create a secure zone for sensitive data, such as financial information, customer records, or intellectual property. This ensures that even if an attacker gains access to one segment of the network, they cannot easily move laterally to access sensitive data.

Furthermore, segmentation can improve network performance and manageability by reducing broadcast domains and isolating traffic. This helps organizations optimize network resources and minimize potential network congestion.

Effective network access control and segmentation require careful planning, policy development, and implementation. Organizations should define clear security policies, including access control rules, authentication methods, and segmentation strategies, to align with their security objectives and risk tolerance.

It is essential to conduct thorough risk assessments to identify potential vulnerabilities and determine the appropriate level of access control and segmentation required. These assessments should consider not only internal risks but also external threats, compliance requirements, and industry-specific regulations.

The selection and deployment of NAC solutions and segmentation techniques should align with the organization's unique requirements and infrastructure. This may involve implementing NAC appliances, software solutions, or utilizing existing network infrastructure for segmentation.

Security policies, access controls, and segmentation rules should be regularly reviewed and updated to adapt to evolving threats and changes in the network environment. Additionally, monitoring and logging play a crucial role in detecting and responding to security incidents within segmented network environments.

User education and awareness are integral to the success of network access control and segmentation initiatives. Employees and users should be educated about security policies, the importance of strong authentication, and the reasons behind network segmentation to foster a culture of security.

In summary, network access control and segmentation are essential strategies for enhancing network security and reducing the attack surface. These approaches enable organizations to regulate and manage access to their networks, ensuring that only authorized devices and users can connect. By implementing NAC and segmentation effectively, organizations can significantly strengthen their cybersecurity defenses and better protect their digital assets from a wide range of threats.

Chapter 6: Protecting Against Malware and Viruses

Malware, short for malicious software, encompasses a diverse and ever-evolving category of software programs designed with malicious intent, posing significant threats to the security and privacy of computer systems and their users. These malicious programs vary in types, characteristics, and functionalities, making them a constant challenge for cybersecurity professionals and organizations worldwide.

One of the most prevalent types of malware is viruses, which are self-replicating programs that attach themselves to legitimate files or software. When infected files are executed, the virus spreads to other files and may perform various malicious actions, such as corrupting data or stealing sensitive information.

Worms are a subset of malware that, unlike viruses, can self-replicate without attaching to existing files. Worms spread across networks and devices, exploiting vulnerabilities to infect as many systems as possible. They can have a significant impact on network performance and may be used for launching coordinated attacks.

Trojan horses, often referred to as Trojans, are deceptive malware programs that disguise themselves as legitimate software or files. When users unknowingly execute them, Trojans grant attackers unauthorized access to the infected system, allowing them to steal data, monitor activities, or initiate other malicious actions.

Ransomware is a particularly destructive type of malware that encrypts a victim's files or entire system and demands a ransom in exchange for the decryption key. Ransomware attacks have targeted individuals, businesses, and even critical infrastructure, causing financial losses and disrupting operations.

Spyware is designed to covertly collect information about a user's activities, such as browsing habits, keystrokes, and personal data, without the user's consent. This stolen information is often used for identity theft, fraud, or espionage purposes.

Adware is a type of malware that primarily aims to display unwanted advertisements to users. While not as destructive as other malware types, adware can be highly annoying and may lead to privacy concerns if it tracks user behavior without consent.

Rootkits are stealthy malware programs that embed themselves deep within an operating system, making them challenging to detect and remove. Rootkits often grant attackers privileged access to a compromised system, allowing them to control it without being detected.

Botnets consist of a network of compromised computers or devices, known as "bots" or "zombies," that are under the control of a central attacker or controller. These botnets can be used to carry out coordinated attacks, such as Distributed Denial of Service (DDoS) attacks, steal data, or distribute other forms of malware.

Keyloggers are malicious programs that record a user's keystrokes, capturing sensitive information like login credentials, credit card numbers, and personal messages. Cybercriminals use keyloggers to steal valuable data for financial gain or identity theft.

Fileless malware is a sophisticated type of malware that operates without leaving traditional traces on a victim's computer. Instead of relying on files or executable code, fileless malware leverages legitimate system processes and memory to execute malicious activities, making detection and removal more challenging.

Polymorphic malware is designed to constantly change its code or appearance to evade traditional signature-based antivirus and anti-malware tools. This adaptability makes it difficult for security solutions to recognize and block polymorphic malware.

Macro malware exploits the macro scripting capabilities in document files, such as Microsoft Word or Excel documents, to execute malicious code when the document is opened. These macros can deliver various payloads, including ransomware or Trojans.

Malvertising, short for malicious advertising, involves the use of online advertisements to deliver malware to users' devices. Cybercriminals inject malicious code into ads that, when clicked or viewed, lead to malware infections.

Mobile malware specifically targets smartphones and tablets, often through malicious apps or infected files. These mobile threats can steal personal data, send premium-rate SMS messages, or turn infected devices into part of a botnet.

Characteristics of malware can vary widely, but they often share common traits such as the ability to conceal themselves from detection, exploit vulnerabilities in software or systems, and execute malicious actions without user consent or knowledge.

Some malware is designed with a specific purpose, such as data exfiltration, financial theft, or system disruption, while others may have multiple functionalities, making them versatile tools for cybercriminals.

Malware can propagate through various means, including email attachments, infected software downloads, malicious links, removable media, and exploiting software vulnerabilities. Social engineering tactics, such as phishing emails or deceptive websites, are frequently used to trick users into downloading or executing malware.

To combat the evolving threat landscape, cybersecurity professionals employ a range of techniques and technologies, including antivirus software, intrusion detection systems, network monitoring, and user education, to detect, prevent, and mitigate the impact of malware attacks.

In summary, malware encompasses a wide array of malicious software programs, each with its own characteristics and purposes. Understanding the various types of malware and their traits is essential for organizations and individuals to protect themselves against these persistent and evolving threats. As cybercriminals continue to innovate, effective cybersecurity measures and vigilant practices remain critical in mitigating the risks posed by malware.

Anti-malware strategies and best practices are essential components of modern cybersecurity efforts, aimed at protecting computer systems, networks, and data from the ever-present threat of malware. These strategies encompass a range of proactive measures and reactive techniques that individuals and organizations can employ to defend against the diverse and evolving landscape of malicious software.

One of the fundamental best practices in anti-malware strategy is the use of reputable antivirus and anti-malware software. These security solutions are designed to detect, quarantine, and remove malicious software from a computer or network, providing a critical first line of defense against malware threats.

Regularly updating antivirus and anti-malware software is crucial to ensure that the security tools have the latest threat definitions and detection capabilities. Cybercriminals constantly develop new malware variants, so staying up-to-date is essential to effectively combat emerging threats.

In addition to antivirus software, organizations should implement intrusion detection and prevention systems (IDPS) to monitor network traffic for suspicious or malicious activities. IDPS can identify patterns indicative of malware attacks and take proactive measures to block or mitigate threats in real-time.

User education and awareness play a vital role in anti-malware strategies. Training employees and users about the dangers of malware, phishing attacks, and best practices for safe online behavior can reduce the likelihood of falling victim to malware-driven social engineering schemes.

Another important best practice is to regularly backup critical data. In the event of a malware infection, having up-to-date backups ensures that valuable information can be restored without paying ransom or suffering data loss. Backup systems should be isolated from the network to prevent malware from compromising them.

Secure web browsing and email practices are essential to avoid malware infections. Users should exercise caution when clicking on links or downloading attachments from unknown or suspicious sources. Employing email filtering and web filtering solutions can help block malicious content before it reaches users' inboxes or browsers.

Network segmentation is a proactive measure that can limit the spread of malware in the event of a breach. By dividing a network into isolated segments with strict access controls, organizations can contain malware and prevent it from moving laterally across the network.

Application whitelisting is a strategy that restricts the execution of software to a predefined list of approved applications. This approach prevents unauthorized or malicious software from running on a system, reducing the attack surface.

Patch management is a critical aspect of anti-malware strategy. Organizations should regularly apply security patches and updates to operating systems, software, and applications to address known vulnerabilities that malware often exploits. Automated patch management tools can streamline this process.

Implementing multi-factor authentication (MFA) adds an additional layer of security by requiring users to provide multiple forms of verification before gaining access to sensitive systems or data. This can prevent unauthorized access even if malware compromises user credentials.

Security information and event management (SIEM) systems help organizations collect, correlate, and analyze security-related data from various sources, including logs and network traffic. SIEM solutions provide insights into potential malware incidents and security breaches, allowing for timely responses.

Continuous monitoring and network traffic analysis can help detect anomalies and patterns indicative of malware activity. Behavioral analysis and anomaly detection technologies can identify unusual or suspicious behavior that may be associated with malware infections.

Incident response plans and procedures are essential components of anti-malware strategies. Organizations should have well-defined incident response plans in place, outlining the steps to take when malware is detected. These plans should include communication protocols, containment measures, and recovery strategies.

Regular security audits and vulnerability assessments help identify weaknesses in an organization's security posture. Penetration testing can simulate real-world attacks to assess how well an organization can defend against malware and other threats.

Security hygiene practices, such as disabling unnecessary services, removing or disabling unused software, and applying the principle of least privilege, help reduce the attack surface and limit the opportunities for malware to exploit vulnerabilities.

Security updates should not be limited to software and systems; firmware and hardware updates are equally important. Ensuring that routers, switches, and other network infrastructure components have up-to-date firmware can prevent malware from exploiting vulnerabilities in these devices.

Network monitoring and analysis can provide insights into malware infections and their behavior within an organization's network. Identifying the indicators of compromise (IoC) and tactics, techniques, and procedures (TTPs) associated with malware can aid in early detection and response.

Collaboration with external cybersecurity organizations, information sharing groups, and industry peers can provide valuable threat intelligence and insights into emerging malware threats. Staying informed about the latest developments in the threat landscape is crucial for adapting anti-malware strategies.

In summary, anti-malware strategies and best practices are essential for defending against the pervasive and constantly evolving threat of malicious software. These strategies encompass a range of proactive and reactive measures, including the use of reputable security software, user education, patch management, and incident response planning. By implementing these practices and staying vigilant, individuals and organizations can enhance their cybersecurity defenses and reduce the risk of falling victim to malware attacks.

Chapter 7: User Authentication and Access Control

User authentication methods and protocols are critical components of modern cybersecurity, serving as the first line of defense against unauthorized access to sensitive information and systems. Authentication is the process of verifying the identity of a user or entity attempting to gain access to a computer system, application, or network.

One of the most commonly used authentication methods is the use of usernames and passwords. Users provide a unique username and a secret password to gain access to their accounts. However, this method has vulnerabilities, such as the risk of weak or easily guessable passwords, password reuse, and the potential for passwords to be stolen through phishing or other attacks.

To enhance the security of username and password authentication, organizations often enforce password policies that require users to create strong, complex passwords and change them regularly. Additionally, multi-factor authentication (MFA) is a widely adopted practice that requires users to provide two or more forms of verification before granting access. This can include something the user knows (password), something the user has (a mobile device or security token), or something the user is (biometric data like fingerprints or facial recognition).

Biometric authentication methods are becoming increasingly prevalent, leveraging unique physiological or behavioral characteristics to verify a user's identity. Biometric authentication includes fingerprint recognition, facial recognition, iris scanning, and voice recognition. These methods offer a high level of security, as they are difficult to impersonate or replicate.

Smart cards and security tokens are hardware-based authentication methods that require users to insert a physical card or token into a reader or connect it to a device. These devices generate one-time passwords (OTPs) or cryptographic keys that are used for authentication. Smart cards are often used for physical and logical access control in government and corporate environments.

Public Key Infrastructure (PKI) is a widely adopted authentication protocol that uses asymmetric cryptography. In PKI, users have a pair of cryptographic keys: a public key and a private key. The public key is freely available, while the private key is kept secret. Authentication occurs when a user presents their public key, and the system verifies it using a corresponding private key stored securely.

Remote authentication protocols, such as Remote Authentication Dial-In User Service (RADIUS) and Lightweight Directory Access Protocol (LDAP), are commonly used in network environments to authenticate users who access resources remotely. RADIUS, for example, authenticates users when they connect to a network, while LDAP is used to authenticate users against a directory service like Microsoft Active Directory.

Single Sign-On (SSO) is a user authentication method that allows users to access multiple applications and services with a single set of credentials. Once authenticated to one application, users are automatically granted access to others without the need to enter their credentials repeatedly. SSO simplifies the user experience and reduces the risk of weak or reused passwords.

Security Assertion Markup Language (SAML) is a widely adopted authentication and authorization protocol used in web-based Single Sign-On (SSO) solutions. SAML enables the exchange of authentication and authorization data between identity providers and service providers, allowing users to access multiple services without sharing their credentials with each service individually.

OAuth (Open Authorization) is a protocol used for delegated authorization, often seen in scenarios where a user wants to grant a third-party application limited access to their resources without disclosing their credentials. OAuth allows users to grant permissions to applications without sharing their passwords.

Multi-Step and Adaptive Authentication are authentication methods that dynamically adjust the authentication process based on risk factors and user behavior. These methods evaluate the context of the authentication request, such as the user's location, device, and behavior, and require additional verification steps when unusual or high-risk conditions are detected.

Device-based authentication leverages the characteristics and security features of a user's device to verify their identity. This includes device fingerprinting, which analyzes unique attributes of the device, and device attestation, which verifies that the device meets certain security requirements before granting access.

Token-based authentication involves the use of cryptographic tokens or certificates to verify a user's identity. Tokens are generated by a trusted authority and are used to provide secure authentication and authorization. This method is commonly used in mobile app authentication and secure web communication.

Authentication protocols, such as Kerberos and OAuth, facilitate the secure exchange of authentication information between parties. Kerberos is a network authentication protocol that uses symmetric key cryptography to authenticate users, while OAuth is a protocol for authorization that enables third-party applications to access a user's resources with their consent.

Federated authentication is a method that allows users to access resources across multiple domains or organizations using a single set of credentials. This is achieved through trust relationships established between identity providers and service providers, enabling seamless authentication and authorization.

User self-service password reset is a method that empowers users to reset their passwords independently, reducing the burden on IT support teams and improving user satisfaction. This typically involves users answering security questions or receiving verification codes via email or SMS.

Continuous authentication is an emerging method that continually monitors user behavior and context throughout a session to detect anomalies or signs of compromise. If unusual behavior is detected, additional authentication steps may be required to verify the user's identity.

In summary, user authentication methods and protocols are essential elements of modern cybersecurity, providing the means to verify the identity of users and entities accessing computer systems, applications, and networks. The choice of authentication method should align with the specific security requirements and risk tolerance of an organization or application. As cyber threats continue to evolve, organizations must implement robust and adaptive authentication mechanisms to protect their digital assets and user data effectively.

Effective access control strategies are fundamental to safeguarding sensitive data, resources, and systems, ensuring that only authorized individuals or entities are granted access while preventing unauthorized or malicious access. Access control is a foundational principle in cybersecurity, encompassing a range of techniques and strategies that govern who can access what, when, and how within an organization's network or physical premises.

Role-based access control (RBAC) is a widely adopted access control strategy that assigns permissions and access rights to users based on their roles and responsibilities within an organization. RBAC simplifies access management by grouping users into predefined roles, such as "employees," "managers," or "administrators," and granting them access rights appropriate to their roles.

Attribute-based access control (ABAC) is a flexible access control model that takes into account various attributes, including user characteristics, resource properties, and environmental conditions, to determine access permissions. ABAC allows for fine-grained access control decisions based on dynamic factors, making it suitable for complex and dynamic environments.

Mandatory Access Control (MAC) is a security model commonly used in highly secure environments, such as government and military systems. MAC enforces access control policies based on labels and security classifications, ensuring that data and resources are protected from unauthorized access, even when users have legitimate access to the system.

Discretionary Access Control (DAC) is a more flexible access control model that allows resource owners to determine access permissions. In DAC, users have control over the resources they own, including the ability to grant or revoke access to others. While DAC provides flexibility, it can lead to security risks if resource owners make improper access decisions.

Rule-Based Access Control (RBAC) is an access control model that uses predefined rules or policies to determine access permissions. RBAC rules are typically based on conditions and criteria defined by administrators, allowing for automated and consistent access control decisions.

Time-based access control is a strategy that restricts access to resources based on predefined time windows or schedules. This approach is often used to limit access to sensitive data or systems during specific hours or days, reducing the exposure to potential threats.

Role-based access control is often implemented using access control lists (ACLs) or access control matrices (ACMs), which define the permissions associated with each role or user. ACLs list the users or roles that have access to a specific resource and the type of access they are granted, such as read, write, or execute permissions.

Access control policies should be regularly reviewed and updated to ensure they align with the organization's security requirements and compliance regulations. This includes removing unnecessary or outdated permissions, adjusting access levels, and validating user roles and attributes.

User provisioning and deprovisioning processes are critical in effective access control. User provisioning involves granting appropriate access rights and permissions to new users, while deprovisioning ensures that access is promptly revoked when users leave the organization or change roles.

Access control mechanisms can be implemented at various layers of an organization's technology stack, including the physical layer, network layer, operating system layer, and application layer. Each layer may require different access control strategies and technologies to protect resources effectively.

In physical access control, measures such as biometric authentication, access cards, and security badges are used to restrict physical entry to buildings, data centers, or restricted areas. Physical access control is essential for protecting physical assets and sensitive equipment.

Network access control (NAC) solutions enforce access policies at the network level, verifying the identity and security posture of devices and users before granting access to the network. NAC can prevent unauthorized devices from connecting to the network and ensure that compliant devices meet security standards.

Operating system-level access control mechanisms, such as discretionary access control lists (DACLs) and mandatory access control (MAC) policies, determine which users or processes can access files, directories, and system resources. These mechanisms are essential for securing the operating system and maintaining data integrity.

Application-level access control governs access to software applications, databases, and web services. Role-based access control, attribute-based access control, and fine-grained access controls are often implemented within applications to manage user permissions and data access.

Access control should be combined with strong authentication methods to ensure that users are who they claim to be. Multi-factor authentication (MFA) adds an extra layer of security by requiring users to provide multiple forms of verification before gaining access.

Access control audits and monitoring play a crucial role in maintaining the security of access controls. Organizations should regularly review access logs, monitor user activities, and conduct access control assessments to identify potential vulnerabilities and unauthorized access.

Regular employee training and awareness programs are essential to educate users about access control policies, the importance of safeguarding access credentials, and reporting suspicious activities. Users should be aware of their role in maintaining the security of access controls.

Effective access control strategies consider the principle of least privilege (PoLP), which grants users or processes only the minimum level of access required to perform their tasks. By following PoLP, organizations reduce the risk of unintended data exposure and privilege escalation.

Security Information and Event Management (SIEM) systems can provide centralized visibility into access control events, allowing organizations to detect and respond to unauthorized access attempts and security incidents in real-time.

Access control policies should be aligned with industry-specific regulations and compliance standards, such as the Health Insurance Portability and Accountability Act (HIPAA) or the Payment Card Industry Data Security Standard (PCI DSS). Ensuring compliance helps protect sensitive data and avoid legal and financial consequences.

In summary, effective access control strategies are essential for organizations to protect their data, systems, and resources from unauthorized access and potential security breaches. These strategies encompass a range of access control models and mechanisms, including RBAC, ABAC, MAC, and DAC, each tailored to the organization's specific security requirements and risk tolerance. By implementing robust access control measures, organizations can mitigate security risks and ensure that only authorized users have access to critical assets and information.

Chapter 8: Data Protection and Encryption

Data protection strategies and encryption play a crucial role in safeguarding sensitive information and ensuring the privacy and security of data in an increasingly digital world. As organizations and individuals rely on digital data for various purposes, from business operations to personal communication, the need to protect this data from unauthorized access, theft, or exposure has become paramount.

Encryption is a fundamental component of data protection strategies, as it involves the transformation of data into a format that is unreadable without the appropriate decryption key. This process ensures that even if unauthorized individuals or entities gain access to the encrypted data, they cannot decipher its contents without the necessary encryption keys.

The importance of encryption lies in its ability to provide confidentiality, integrity, and authentication for data. When data is encrypted, it becomes unreadable to anyone who does not possess the decryption key, effectively preventing unauthorized access and eavesdropping.

Moreover, encryption ensures data integrity by detecting any unauthorized changes or tampering attempts. When data is decrypted, the decryption process verifies that the data has not been altered since it was originally encrypted. If any changes are detected, it raises a red flag, indicating potential tampering or data corruption.

Authentication is another critical aspect of encryption. Encryption keys serve as a means of verifying the identity of both the sender and the recipient of encrypted data. This authentication process helps ensure that data is transmitted or accessed only by authorized parties, reducing the risk of data breaches. Data protection strategies often involve the use of encryption at various stages of data handling, including data storage, data transmission, and data processing. Full-disk encryption, for example, encrypts the entire storage device or disk, protecting data at rest. This prevents unauthorized access to data if the physical storage device is lost, stolen, or compromised.

In contrast, data in transit encryption focuses on securing data while it is being transmitted over networks or between devices. Transport Layer Security (TLS) and Secure Sockets Layer (SSL) are common encryption protocols used to protect data during internet communication, such as when browsing websites or sending emails.

End-to-end encryption is a particularly robust form of encryption used in messaging apps and communication services. With end-to-end encryption, data is encrypted on the sender's device and can only be decrypted by the intended recipient. This ensures that even service providers cannot access the contents of the messages.

File-level encryption is another data protection strategy that allows individual files or documents to be encrypted separately. Users can encrypt specific files containing sensitive information, providing an extra layer of security for critical data.

While encryption is a powerful tool for data protection, it is essential to manage encryption keys effectively. Encryption keys are the linchpin of the encryption process, and losing or mishandling them can lead to data loss or unavailability.

Key management practices involve generating, storing, distributing, and revoking encryption keys securely. Organizations must establish robust key management policies and procedures to safeguard keys against theft or compromise. Hardware security modules (HSMs) and key management systems (KMS) are often used to protect and manage encryption keys.

Data classification is another fundamental component of data protection strategies. By classifying data based on its sensitivity and importance, organizations can prioritize encryption efforts. Highly sensitive data, such as financial records or personal health information, may require stronger encryption measures than less sensitive data, such as publicly available information.

Data protection also extends to data backup and disaster recovery strategies. Regularly backing up data and ensuring that backups are encrypted is crucial for ensuring data availability and recoverability in the event of data loss or system failures.

Data encryption is not limited to organizational data; it also applies to personal data protection. Individuals can encrypt their files, devices, and communications to protect their privacy and sensitive information from unauthorized access or interception.

One common example of personal data encryption is encrypting smartphones and laptops to prevent unauthorized access to personal photos, emails, and documents. Mobile device encryption ensures that if a device is lost or stolen, the data remains protected.

Another example is email encryption, which allows individuals to send and receive encrypted emails to protect the confidentiality of their communication. Secure email services and encryption plugins offer users the ability to encrypt email content and attachments.

Password managers are valuable tools for individuals to protect their login credentials and sensitive information. Passwords stored in password managers are typically encrypted with strong encryption algorithms, adding an extra layer of security to user accounts.

Data protection regulations and compliance requirements, such as the General Data Protection Regulation (GDPR) and the Health Insurance Portability and Accountability Act (HIPAA), often mandate the use of encryption to protect sensitive data. Organizations must adhere to these regulations to avoid legal and financial consequences.

In summary, data protection strategies and encryption are indispensable components of cybersecurity, providing confidentiality, integrity, and authentication for data. Encryption plays a pivotal role in safeguarding data at rest, in transit, and during processing. Effective key management, data classification, and backup strategies enhance data protection efforts, while compliance with data protection regulations is essential for organizations and individuals alike. As digital data continues to be a valuable asset, investing in robust data protection measures is crucial to ensure its security and privacy. Encryption techniques and algorithms are at the heart of data security, providing a critical layer of protection against unauthorized access and eavesdropping. These cryptographic methods transform data into an unreadable format, rendering it inaccessible to anyone without the proper decryption key. One of the fundamental encryption techniques is symmetric encryption, also known as private-key encryption, where the same key is used for both encryption and decryption. Symmetric encryption algorithms, such as Advanced Encryption Standard (AES) and Data Encryption Standard (DES), are efficient and suitable for encrypting large volumes of data.

Symmetric encryption relies on a shared secret key, making it essential to securely exchange the key between the sender and the recipient. The security of symmetric encryption hinges on safeguarding this key from unauthorized access.

Asymmetric encryption, on the other hand, employs a pair of mathematically related keys: a public key for encryption and a private key for decryption. This approach, also known as public-key encryption, offers greater security and eliminates the need for secure key exchange.

Public-key encryption is widely used in secure communication protocols like Transport Layer Security (TLS) and Secure Sockets Layer (SSL) to protect data transmitted over the internet. The recipient's public key is used to encrypt the data, and only the recipient, who possesses the corresponding private key, can decrypt it.

Public-key infrastructure (PKI) is an essential framework for managing public and private keys in asymmetric encryption. PKI systems generate and distribute digital certificates that verify the authenticity of public keys, ensuring that users are communicating with trusted parties.

Hybrid encryption combines both symmetric and asymmetric encryption to harness the strengths of each approach. In hybrid encryption, data is first encrypted using a symmetric key, and then the symmetric key is encrypted using the recipient's public key. This allows for efficient data encryption with the security benefits of asymmetric encryption.

Block ciphers and stream ciphers are two categories of symmetric encryption algorithms. Block ciphers encrypt data in fixed-size blocks, typically 64 or 128 bits at a time, making them suitable for encrypting structured data. AES is a widely adopted block cipher known for its security and efficiency.

Stream ciphers, on the other hand, encrypt data one bit or byte at a time, making them suitable for encrypting real-time communication streams like voice or video. RC4 is an example of a stream cipher.

The security of encryption algorithms depends on the key length and the strength of the encryption method. Longer encryption keys offer greater security by increasing the number of possible keys that an attacker must try to break the encryption.

Cryptanalysis is the practice of attempting to decipher encrypted data without the decryption key. The security of encryption algorithms relies on their resistance to cryptanalysis techniques, such as brute force attacks, where an attacker systematically tries all possible keys.

Advanced Encryption Standard (AES) is a symmetric encryption algorithm widely used to secure data. AES operates on fixed-size blocks of data and supports key lengths of 128, 192, or 256 bits. It has withstood extensive cryptanalysis and is considered highly secure.

Data Encryption Standard (DES) was one of the earliest symmetric encryption algorithms, but its 56-bit key length was deemed insufficient for modern security needs. Triple DES (3DES) is an enhancement that applies the DES algorithm three times with different keys to improve security.

Rivest Cipher (RC) is a family of stream ciphers developed by Ron Rivest. RC4, in particular, gained popularity but is now considered insecure due to vulnerabilities. RC4 should be avoided in favor of more secure encryption algorithms.

RSA, named after its inventors Ron Rivest, Adi Shamir, and Leonard Adleman, is one of the most widely used asymmetric encryption algorithms. RSA relies on the difficulty of factoring large composite numbers, making it computationally challenging to derive the private key from the public key.

Elliptic Curve Cryptography (ECC) is an asymmetric encryption technique that offers strong security with shorter key lengths compared to traditional asymmetric encryption algorithms like RSA. ECC is increasingly used in secure communication and digital signatures.

Diffie-Hellman key exchange is a cryptographic protocol that allows two parties to securely exchange cryptographic keys over an insecure communication channel. It forms the basis of many secure communication protocols, such as TLS and SSL.

Quantum computing poses a potential threat to existing encryption algorithms, as it has the potential to break widely used encryption methods by quickly factoring large numbers. Post-quantum cryptography research is ongoing to develop encryption techniques resistant to quantum attacks.

Hash functions are cryptographic algorithms that generate a fixed-size output, known as a hash value or digest, from input data of arbitrary size. Hash functions are used in data integrity verification and password hashing.

The security of hash functions relies on properties such as collision resistance, where it is computationally infeasible to find two different inputs that produce the same hash value. SHA-256 (part of the SHA-2 family) and SHA-3 are widely used cryptographic hash functions.

Message Authentication Codes (MACs) are used to verify the authenticity and integrity of a message. A MAC is generated using a secret key and the message itself. Recipients can verify the message's integrity by re-computing the MAC and comparing it to the received MAC.

In summary, encryption techniques and algorithms are essential tools in securing digital data and communication. Whether through symmetric encryption, asymmetric encryption, or hybrid encryption, cryptographic methods provide confidentiality, integrity, and authentication for data in various contexts, from secure messaging to protecting sensitive information. As encryption continues to evolve to counter emerging threats, it remains a cornerstone of modern cybersecurity.

Chapter 9: Incident Response and Recovery

Incident response planning and preparation are critical components of an organization's cybersecurity strategy, aimed at effectively managing and mitigating security incidents when they occur. In today's digital landscape, where cyber threats are constantly evolving, having a well-defined incident response plan is essential to minimize damage, protect data, and maintain business continuity.

An incident response plan outlines the procedures and actions to be taken when a security incident is detected. It provides a structured approach for identifying, containing, eradicating, and recovering from security incidents while preserving evidence for investigation and compliance purposes.

The first step in incident response planning is establishing an incident response team. This team typically includes representatives from various departments, including IT, legal, compliance, and communication, to ensure a comprehensive and coordinated response to incidents.

The incident response team should be trained and equipped to handle various types of incidents, from data breaches and malware infections to denial-of-service attacks and insider threats. Regular training and tabletop exercises help the team understand their roles and responsibilities and improve their response efficiency.

Incident classification is a crucial aspect of incident response planning. Security incidents are categorized based on their severity, impact, and potential harm to the organization. These categories help prioritize incident response efforts and allocate resources accordingly.

Incident detection is the process of identifying security incidents as they occur or shortly after. Advanced threat detection tools, intrusion detection systems, security information and event management (SIEM) solutions, and log analysis play vital roles in timely incident detection.

Upon detection of a security incident, it is crucial to assess the situation promptly. The incident response team must determine the scope, impact, and potential consequences of the incident to make informed decisions about containment and mitigation.

Containment is the immediate action taken to prevent the incident from spreading further. This may involve isolating affected systems, disabling compromised accounts, or blocking malicious network traffic to limit the incident's reach.

Eradication is the process of identifying and removing the root cause of the incident to prevent it from recurring. This may involve patching vulnerabilities, removing malware, or closing security gaps in the organization's infrastructure.

After containment and eradication, the incident response team focuses on recovery efforts. Recovery aims to restore affected systems and services to normal operation. Backups and disaster recovery plans are essential in this phase to minimize downtime and data loss.

Communication is a critical element of incident response planning. Effective communication ensures that all stakeholders, including employees, customers, partners, and regulators, are informed about the incident's status, impact, and resolution efforts.

Legal and compliance considerations are also vital in incident response planning. Organizations must adhere to data breach notification laws and industry-specific regulations when a security incident involves the exposure of sensitive data. Legal counsel can provide guidance on regulatory compliance and potential liabilities.

Preservation of evidence is essential for post-incident analysis and potential legal proceedings. Incident response teams should follow documented procedures to collect, secure, and document evidence related to the incident.

Public relations and reputation management are critical during and after a security incident. Organizations must craft a consistent and transparent message for external stakeholders to maintain trust and credibility.

Post-incident analysis, also known as a post-mortem or lessons learned, is an essential step in incident response planning. The incident response team reviews the incident's handling to identify areas for improvement and refine the incident response plan.

Incident response planning is not a one-time effort; it should be an ongoing and iterative process. As the threat landscape evolves and technology changes, incident response plans must be updated to address new risks and vulnerabilities.

Threat intelligence plays a significant role in incident response planning and preparation. Organizations should have access to up-to-date threat intelligence feeds and information sharing networks to stay informed about emerging threats and attack trends.

Collaboration with external parties, such as incident response vendors, law enforcement, and industry-specific Information Sharing and Analysis Centers (ISACs), can enhance incident response capabilities and provide access to additional resources and expertise.

In addition to technical aspects, incident response planning should also consider the human factor. Employees should be educated and aware of their roles in incident reporting and response, as well as best practices for preventing security incidents.

An incident response plan should include clear incident reporting procedures. Employees should know how to report suspicious activities or incidents to the incident response team promptly.

Regular testing and simulation exercises, such as red teaming and penetration testing, are valuable for evaluating the effectiveness of an incident response plan and identifying weaknesses that need improvement.

Incident response planning should align with an organization's risk management strategy. It should prioritize incidents based on their potential impact and ensure that the most critical assets and systems receive the highest level of protection and attention.

In summary, incident response planning and preparation are essential components of a comprehensive cybersecurity strategy. A well-structured incident response plan helps organizations effectively manage and mitigate security incidents, protect sensitive data, and maintain business continuity. It involves various stages, from detection and containment to recovery and post-incident analysis, and should be continuously updated to adapt to evolving threats and technologies. With the right planning and a proactive approach, organizations can better defend against cyber threats and respond decisively when incidents occur.

Incident recovery processes are a crucial part of the incident response lifecycle, aiming to restore normalcy after a security incident and prevent its recurrence. While incident response focuses on containing and mitigating the incident, recovery focuses on returning affected systems and services to their pre-incident state and improving security measures to prevent similar incidents in the future.

The incident recovery process begins after the incident has been contained and eradicated. During this phase, organizations assess the extent of the damage and determine the steps needed to recover fully. Incident recovery plans, which are part of the overall incident response plan, provide a structured framework for these efforts.

Recovery efforts often start with the restoration of affected systems and services. Backup and disaster recovery procedures are crucial in this phase, as they ensure that organizations can quickly recover data and configurations to minimize downtime and data loss.

Organizations must prioritize which systems and services to restore first based on their criticality to business operations. Business impact assessments conducted as part of the incident response planning process help identify these critical systems and prioritize their recovery.

Communication is essential throughout the incident recovery process. Organizations must keep stakeholders, both internal and external, informed about the progress of recovery efforts. This includes employees, customers, partners, regulators, and the public when necessary.

Legal and compliance considerations continue to be important during incident recovery. Organizations must ensure that they comply with data breach notification laws and industry-specific regulations if the incident involves the exposure of sensitive data. Legal counsel may provide guidance on regulatory requirements and liabilities.

Preservation of evidence is also crucial during the recovery phase, as it may be needed for post-incident analysis, regulatory compliance, or legal proceedings. Organizations should follow documented procedures to collect, secure, and document evidence related to the incident.

Public relations and reputation management are integral to the recovery phase. Organizations must craft a consistent and transparent message for external stakeholders to maintain trust and credibility. Rebuilding the organization's reputation may take time, but open communication and a commitment to improving security can help.

Post-incident analysis, often referred to as a post-mortem or lessons learned, is a vital component of incident recovery. The incident response team reviews how the incident was handled, identifies areas for improvement, and refines the incident response plan based on lessons learned.

Post-incident analysis involves a thorough examination of the incident's timeline, from initial detection to containment and recovery. It identifies what went well during the response and what could have been done better.

During the post-incident analysis, organizations should assess the effectiveness of their incident response procedures, the performance of the incident response team, and the impact of the incident on business operations.

An important aspect of the post-incident analysis is identifying root causes and contributing factors that led to the incident. Understanding these factors is essential for preventing similar incidents in the future.

Root cause analysis techniques, such as the "5 Whys" method or the Fishbone (Ishikawa) diagram, can help organizations delve deeper into the underlying issues that allowed the incident to occur.

Once root causes and contributing factors are identified, organizations can develop corrective and preventive actions (CAPAs) to address these issues and improve security posture. CAPAs may include changes to policies and procedures, security controls, employee training, or technology investments.

Implementing CAPAs is an integral part of the recovery phase, as it helps organizations build resilience and reduce the risk of future incidents. It's crucial to assign responsibility for implementing CAPAs and establish timelines for completion.

Regularly reviewing and updating the incident response plan is another outcome of the post-incident analysis. The plan should be adjusted to incorporate lessons learned from the incident, including changes in procedures, roles, and responsibilities.

Continuous improvement is a key principle in incident recovery processes. Organizations should not view incidents solely as disruptions but as opportunities to strengthen their security posture and response capabilities.

Incident recovery should also include efforts to enhance incident detection and prevention mechanisms. Strengthening security controls, monitoring, and threat intelligence can help organizations identify and mitigate threats more effectively.

Collaboration with external parties, such as incident response vendors, industry-specific Information Sharing and Analysis Centers (ISACs), and law enforcement, can provide valuable insights and resources for incident recovery and future prevention efforts.

In summary, incident recovery processes are integral to the incident response lifecycle, focusing on restoring normalcy and improving security measures after a security incident. Recovery efforts involve system and service restoration, communication with stakeholders, legal and compliance considerations, evidence preservation, public relations, and post-incident analysis. Lessons learned from incidents should drive continuous improvement in an organization's security posture, with a focus on preventing similar incidents in the future. By taking a proactive and learning-oriented approach, organizations can better protect themselves against evolving cyber threats.

Chapter 10: Developing a Resilient Cybersecurity Strategy

Frameworks for cybersecurity strategy development are essential tools that organizations can leverage to establish a structured and comprehensive approach to safeguarding their digital assets and data in an increasingly interconnected and threat-filled landscape. These frameworks provide a blueprint for assessing risks, defining objectives, implementing security measures, and continuously monitoring and improving cybersecurity posture.

One such widely adopted framework is the NIST Cybersecurity Framework, created by the National Institute of Standards and Technology (NIST) in response to growing cybersecurity challenges. The NIST framework consists of five core functions: Identify, Protect, Detect, Respond, and Recover, providing a systematic approach to managing and mitigating cyber risks.

The "Identify" function focuses on understanding an organization's assets, business processes, and potential risks. It involves asset management, risk assessment, and the development of a risk management strategy.

Asset management within the "Identify" function helps organizations catalog their hardware, software, data, and other digital assets, gaining visibility into their technology ecosystem and understanding what needs protection.

Risk assessment is another critical component of the "Identify" function, where organizations identify and prioritize risks based on their potential impact on business operations. This process informs the development of risk management strategies tailored to an organization's unique needs.

The "Protect" function emphasizes the implementation of security measures to safeguard assets and data from cyber threats. This includes access control, data encryption, security awareness training, and security policies and procedures.

Access control measures restrict unauthorized access to systems and data, ensuring that only authorized personnel can access sensitive information. This includes user authentication, authorization, and the principle of least privilege.

Data encryption is a protective measure that transforms data into an unreadable format, making it inaccessible to unauthorized individuals even if they gain access to the encrypted data.

Security awareness training educates employees about cybersecurity best practices, helping them recognize and respond to potential threats, such as phishing attacks or social engineering attempts.

Security policies and procedures provide guidelines for employees and system administrators to follow, outlining acceptable use, incident reporting, and incident response protocols.

The "Detect" function is focused on identifying and detecting security incidents promptly. This includes continuous monitoring, anomaly detection, and security event logging.

Continuous monitoring involves the real-time monitoring of network traffic, system activities, and user behavior to detect abnormal patterns or suspicious activities.

Anomaly detection techniques use machine learning and statistical analysis to identify deviations from normal behavior and raise alerts when potential security incidents are detected.

Security event logging ensures that detailed records of system and network activities are maintained, facilitating incident investigations and post-incident analysis.

The "Respond" function outlines the steps an organization should take when a security incident occurs. This includes incident response planning, communication, and incident containment.

Incident response planning involves creating a structured framework for managing security incidents, defining roles and responsibilities, and establishing communication channels within the organization.

Communication during an incident is crucial to coordinate response efforts and inform stakeholders about the incident's status, impact, and remediation efforts.

Incident containment is the immediate action taken to prevent the incident from spreading further and causing more damage. It may involve isolating affected systems, disabling compromised accounts, or blocking malicious network traffic.

The "Recover" function focuses on restoring affected systems and services to normal operation after an incident. This includes recovery planning, data backup, and business continuity planning.

Recovery planning outlines the procedures for restoring affected systems and services, prioritizing critical assets to minimize downtime.

Data backup and disaster recovery strategies ensure that organizations can recover data and configurations from backups to minimize data loss and downtime.

Business continuity planning encompasses strategies for maintaining essential business operations during and after a cyber incident, ensuring that the organization can continue to deliver its products or services.

The NIST Cybersecurity Framework provides organizations with a flexible and adaptable approach to cybersecurity strategy development, allowing them to tailor their efforts to their specific needs and risk profiles.

Another notable framework is the ISO/IEC 27001, a globally recognized standard for information security management systems (ISMS). ISO/IEC 27001 provides a systematic and risk-based approach to managing information security, covering processes like risk assessment, risk treatment, and continuous improvement.

The ISO/IEC 27001 framework begins with the identification of an organization's information assets and the assessment of risks related to their confidentiality, integrity, and availability.

Risk treatment involves selecting and implementing security controls and measures to mitigate identified risks to an acceptable level, ensuring the protection of information assets.

The framework also emphasizes the importance of an information security management system (ISMS), a systematic approach to managing and improving information security across the organization.

Other frameworks, such as the CIS Critical Security Controls (CIS Controls), provide a prioritized set of actions that organizations can take to improve their cybersecurity posture. These controls cover areas like inventory and control of hardware assets, continuous vulnerability assessment and remediation, and data protection.

The adoption of cybersecurity frameworks is not limited to large organizations; small and medium-sized enterprises (SMEs) can also benefit from them. Many frameworks offer scalability and adaptability to meet the needs and resources of SMEs, helping them enhance their security posture.

In summary, cybersecurity frameworks provide organizations with structured approaches to assess, protect, detect, respond to, and recover from cyber threats. These frameworks, such as the NIST Cybersecurity Framework, ISO/IEC 27001, and CIS Critical Security Controls, offer guidance and best practices for managing information security and mitigating risks effectively. Organizations can select the framework that best aligns with their goals, risk profile, and resources, helping them develop robust and resilient cybersecurity strategies in an ever-evolving threat landscape.

Creating a robust cybersecurity roadmap is a critical endeavor for organizations looking to strengthen their security posture in an increasingly digital and interconnected world. A cybersecurity roadmap serves as a strategic plan that outlines the organization's vision, goals, and actionable steps to enhance its cybersecurity defenses.

The first step in creating a cybersecurity roadmap is to conduct a comprehensive assessment of the organization's current cybersecurity posture. This assessment should include a thorough examination of existing security policies, practices, technologies, and vulnerabilities.

Identifying assets is a fundamental aspect of the assessment, as organizations need to know what needs protection, including data, systems, applications, and network infrastructure.

The assessment should also consider potential threats and risks that the organization faces, such as cyberattacks, data breaches, and compliance violations. Understanding these risks is essential for tailoring the roadmap to address specific vulnerabilities.

Once the assessment is complete, organizations can define their cybersecurity vision and goals. This vision should align with the organization's overall mission and business objectives, emphasizing the importance of cybersecurity as a strategic enabler.

Goals should be specific, measurable, achievable, relevant, and time-bound (SMART). For example, a goal might be to reduce the number of security incidents by 30% within the next year.

With a clear vision and SMART goals in place, organizations can start building their cybersecurity roadmap. The roadmap outlines the strategic initiatives, projects, and milestones required to achieve the defined goals.

Prioritizing initiatives is a critical step in creating the roadmap, as organizations often have limited resources and need to focus on the most impactful projects first. Prioritization should consider the potential impact on security posture, regulatory requirements, and business continuity.

Cybersecurity initiatives may include upgrading security infrastructure, implementing new security controls, enhancing employee training programs, and developing incident response plans.

It's essential to allocate resources, such as budgets and personnel, to each initiative to ensure successful implementation. Resource allocation should be based on the prioritization of initiatives and the organization's risk appetite.

Project timelines and milestones are another critical component of the cybersecurity roadmap. These timelines help organizations track progress and ensure that initiatives stay on schedule.

Regular review and monitoring of the roadmap are crucial to ensure that it remains aligned with the organization's evolving needs and the changing threat landscape.

Cybersecurity is dynamic, and the roadmap should adapt accordingly.

Cybersecurity roadmaps should also consider emerging technologies and trends that may impact an organization's security posture. This includes the adoption of cloud computing, Internet of Things (IoT) devices, and artificial intelligence (AI) in the organization's IT environment.

To effectively create and implement a cybersecurity roadmap, organizations should establish clear accountability and ownership for each initiative. This includes designating project managers, technical leads, and stakeholders responsible for driving and overseeing the initiatives.

Communication and collaboration are essential throughout the roadmap's implementation. Cross-functional teams, including IT, security, legal, compliance, and business units, should work together to achieve the defined goals.

Measuring and evaluating progress is a critical aspect of the roadmap. Key performance indicators (KPIs) should be established to track the effectiveness of cybersecurity initiatives and the overall security posture.

Regular reporting and feedback loops help stakeholders stay informed about progress and make necessary adjustments to the roadmap as needed.

Budgeting and resource management are vital considerations for the successful execution of the roadmap. Organizations should allocate sufficient resources to support the initiatives and ensure that cybersecurity remains a priority.

As part of the roadmap, organizations should also plan for incident response and recovery. This includes developing incident response plans, conducting tabletop exercises, and ensuring that the organization is prepared to respond effectively to security incidents.

A culture of cybersecurity awareness and education should be fostered within the organization. Employees at all levels should understand their roles and responsibilities in maintaining a secure environment.

Continuous improvement is a fundamental principle of cybersecurity roadmaps. Organizations should regularly assess their security posture, identify areas for improvement, and update the roadmap accordingly.

Regulatory compliance is another important consideration in cybersecurity roadmaps. Organizations must stay informed about relevant laws and regulations that govern data protection and security practices in their industry and geographic region.

Cybersecurity roadmaps should also address third-party risk management. Organizations that rely on vendors and partners should assess their cybersecurity practices and ensure that they align with the organization's security standards.

In summary, creating a robust cybersecurity roadmap is a strategic imperative for organizations seeking to enhance their cybersecurity defenses. The roadmap should begin with a comprehensive assessment of the organization's current posture, followed by the definition of a clear vision, SMART goals, and a prioritized list of initiatives. Collaboration, monitoring, resource management, and continuous improvement are key elements in successfully implementing and maintaining the roadmap. By following a well-defined roadmap, organizations can navigate the evolving threat landscape and bolster their cybersecurity posture to protect critical assets and data.

BOOK 2
MASTERING DEFENSE IN DEPTH
ADVANCED STRATEGIES FOR NETWORK SECURITY AND
CYBER RESILIENCE

ROB BOTWRIGHT

Chapter 1: Evolving Threats in the Digital Age

The landscape of modern cyber threats is a dynamic and ever-evolving ecosystem where malicious actors constantly seek vulnerabilities to exploit and compromise digital assets. In today's interconnected world, individuals, organizations, and governments face an unprecedented array of cyber threats that can have far-reaching consequences.

Cyber threats encompass a wide range of malicious activities, from relatively simple attacks like phishing and malware infections to complex and sophisticated campaigns conducted by nation-state actors. These threats can target individuals, businesses, critical infrastructure, and even entire nations.

One of the most prevalent and persistent cyber threats is phishing, which involves the use of deceptive emails, websites, or messages to trick individuals into revealing sensitive information, such as login credentials or financial data. Phishing attacks have become increasingly sophisticated, making it challenging for users to discern legitimate communication from fraudulent ones.

Malware, short for malicious software, remains a significant threat vector in the cyber landscape. Malware includes viruses, worms, Trojans, ransomware, and spyware, among other types. Malicious actors use malware to gain unauthorized access to systems, steal data, disrupt operations, or extort victims through ransomware attacks.

Ransomware attacks have gained notoriety in recent years as cybercriminals encrypt victims' data and demand a ransom for its release. These attacks have targeted organizations of all sizes, from healthcare institutions and government agencies to private businesses, causing financial losses and operational disruptions.

Advanced Persistent Threats (APTs) represent another category of cyber threats characterized by a high degree of sophistication, stealth, and persistence. APTs are often associated with nation-state actors and are designed to infiltrate and remain undetected within a target's network for extended periods, allowing the attacker to gather intelligence or carry out espionage.

Nation-state-sponsored cyberattacks have garnered significant attention due to their potential for geopolitical impact. These attacks can include the theft of sensitive government data, manipulation of critical infrastructure systems, or the dissemination of disinformation to influence public opinion.

Distributed Denial of Service (DDoS) attacks pose a threat to organizations by overwhelming their online services with a flood of traffic, rendering them inaccessible to legitimate users. DDoS attacks can be used for financial extortion, competitive disruption, or as a diversion tactic during other cyber operations.

Social engineering attacks exploit human psychology and behavior to manipulate individuals into divulging confidential information or performing actions that benefit the attacker. Social engineering tactics may involve pretexting, baiting, tailgating, or spear-phishing, and they often target employees or individuals with access to valuable data.

Insider threats, whether intentional or unintentional, pose a unique challenge to organizations. These threats arise from individuals within an organization who misuse their access to data or systems, either for personal gain or inadvertently due to negligence. Insider threats can result in data breaches or intellectual property theft.

Zero-day vulnerabilities are a concern in the cyber threat landscape. These are software vulnerabilities that are unknown to the software vendor and have no available patches or fixes. Cybercriminals and state-sponsored actors may exploit zero-day vulnerabilities to launch targeted attacks before the vulnerabilities are discovered and patched.

The Internet of Things (IoT) introduces a new dimension to cyber threats. The proliferation of interconnected devices, from smart home appliances to industrial sensors, creates a larger attack surface. Weak security practices in IoT devices can allow attackers to compromise and control them for malicious purposes.

Supply chain attacks have gained prominence as cybercriminals target the software and hardware supply chain to introduce vulnerabilities into products. These attacks can affect a wide range of organizations that rely on third-party suppliers and distributors.

The convergence of cyber and physical threats has become increasingly apparent as critical infrastructure systems, such as power grids, water treatment plants, and transportation networks, become more connected. A cyberattack on critical infrastructure can have severe consequences for public safety and national security.

Cyber threats are not limited to specific industries or sectors; they affect individuals, businesses, governments, and critical infrastructure worldwide. The motivations behind cyber threats vary, including financial gain, espionage, ideological beliefs, and political influence.

The evolving nature of cyber threats requires constant vigilance and proactive cybersecurity measures. Organizations and individuals must adopt a defense-in-depth approach, implementing layers of security controls, regular patch management, employee training, and incident response plans to mitigate the risk of cyberattacks.

Governments and international organizations also play a crucial role in addressing cyber threats through the development of cybersecurity policies, regulations, and international cooperation agreements. These efforts aim to establish norms of responsible behavior in cyberspace and deter malicious actors.

In summary, the landscape of modern cyber threats is multifaceted and continuously evolving. Cybercriminals, nation-states, and other malicious actors employ a variety of tactics, techniques, and procedures to exploit vulnerabilities and target individuals, organizations, and critical infrastructure. Staying informed about emerging threats, adopting robust cybersecurity measures, and fostering international cooperation are essential strategies for mitigating the risks posed by these threats in today's digital age. Threat actors in the cybersecurity landscape are diverse and driven by a wide range of motivations, making it essential to understand their profiles and goals to effectively defend against cyber threats. These actors can vary from individual hackers to organized criminal groups, hacktivists, and nation-states, each with its unique objectives and techniques.

Individual hackers, often referred to as "black hat" hackers, engage in cybercriminal activities for personal gain. Their motivations may include financial profit, such as stealing credit card information, selling stolen data on the dark web, or carrying out ransomware attacks to extort victims. These actors are typically driven by monetary rewards and are known for their skills in exploiting vulnerabilities.

Criminal organizations represent a significant and sophisticated threat in the cyber landscape. These groups are often well-funded and organized, specializing in a range of cybercrimes, including identity theft, fraud, and the distribution of malware. Their motivations are primarily financial, aiming to generate substantial profits through cybercriminal activities.

Hacktivists are individuals or groups with ideological or political motivations who use hacking as a means to advance their causes or beliefs. Their actions may include defacing websites, launching distributed denial of service (DDoS) attacks, or stealing sensitive information to expose perceived injustices or advocate for particular social or political issues. Hacktivism is often characterized by its emphasis on making a public statement rather than monetary gain.

State-sponsored threat actors, also known as Advanced Persistent Threat (APT) groups, are typically associated with nation-states and intelligence agencies. These actors operate with significant resources and advanced capabilities, conducting cyber espionage, data theft, and disruption campaigns to further national interests. Their motivations include gaining a strategic advantage, acquiring intellectual property, or influencing global events.

Cyber espionage actors focus on stealing sensitive information, intellectual property, and government secrets. Their motivations are often linked to espionage, intelligence gathering, and gaining a competitive edge in economic or geopolitical domains. These threat actors can be nation-states, criminal organizations, or hacktivist groups with specific espionage objectives.

Disruptive threat actors aim to disrupt or damage systems and infrastructure for various reasons. These motivations can range from causing chaos and economic damage to advancing a political agenda. Disruptive attacks may include DDoS attacks, targeting critical infrastructure, or spreading malware to disrupt operations.

Nation-state actors engage in cyber activities to further their country's interests and national security objectives. These actors are often well-funded and have access to advanced cyber capabilities. Their motivations may include gathering intelligence, conducting cyber espionage, sabotaging adversaries, or exerting influence on the global stage.

Insiders, such as employees or contractors, pose a unique threat as they have insider knowledge and access to an organization's systems and data. Insider threats can be both malicious and unintentional. Malicious insiders may have motivations like revenge, financial gain, or espionage, while unintentional insiders may inadvertently compromise security through negligence or lack of awareness.

Script kiddies are individuals with limited technical skills who use pre-written scripts or tools to carry out cyberattacks. Their motivations often involve seeking recognition among their peers or causing disruptions for personal satisfaction. Script kiddies are generally less sophisticated than other threat actors but can still pose a threat to vulnerable targets.

The motivations of threat actors can vary widely, from financial gain and ideological beliefs to espionage and geopolitical influence. Understanding these motivations is crucial for organizations and governments when developing cybersecurity strategies and threat mitigation plans.

To defend against cyber threats effectively, organizations must employ a multi-layered approach that includes robust security measures, employee training, incident response plans, and threat intelligence sharing. Collaboration among governments, law enforcement agencies, private sector organizations, and international cybersecurity communities is also essential in combating the diverse and evolving landscape of threat actors and their motivations.

Chapter 2: Advanced Network Architecture for Security

Network design principles play a crucial role in enhancing security in the digital age, where the interconnectedness of devices and systems demands robust protection against a myriad of cyber threats. A well-designed network not only ensures the efficient flow of data and services but also bolsters defenses against potential breaches and attacks.

One fundamental principle in network design for enhanced security is the principle of least privilege (PoLP). This principle dictates that users and systems should only have the minimum level of access necessary to perform their functions, reducing the potential attack surface and limiting the damage that can be caused by compromised accounts.

Network segmentation is another key design principle that can greatly enhance security. By dividing a network into smaller, isolated segments, organizations can contain breaches and limit lateral movement for attackers, preventing them from accessing critical systems or sensitive data.

The concept of defense in depth is foundational to network security design. It involves the implementation of multiple layers of security controls, such as firewalls, intrusion detection systems, and antivirus software, to protect against various attack vectors. This layered approach ensures that even if one layer is breached, others remain intact to thwart attackers.

Implementing strong access controls is essential to network security. This includes measures like strong authentication mechanisms, such as multi-factor authentication (MFA), and robust authorization processes that enforce access policies based on user roles and responsibilities.

Secure network design principles also encompass the use of encryption to protect data in transit and at rest. Encryption protocols, such as Transport Layer Security (TLS) and IPsec, ensure that data is unreadable to unauthorized parties, even if intercepted during transmission.

Secure network protocols and standards, like Secure Sockets Layer (SSL) and Domain Name System Security Extensions (DNSSEC), further enhance security by safeguarding communications and domain name resolution processes against tampering and eavesdropping.

Implementing intrusion detection and prevention systems (IDPS) is crucial for early threat detection and mitigation. IDPS solutions monitor network traffic for suspicious activities and can take automated actions to block or alert on potential threats.

Regular network monitoring and log analysis are essential for identifying abnormal behaviors or security incidents promptly. Continuous monitoring allows organizations to respond quickly to potential threats and minimize the impact of security breaches.

The principle of patch management is integral to network security design. Timely patching of software and firmware vulnerabilities ensures that known vulnerabilities are addressed, reducing the risk of exploitation by attackers.

Network design should also account for the human element in security. This involves user education and awareness training to help individuals recognize and respond to security threats effectively. Educated users are a critical line of defense against phishing attacks and social engineering attempts.

Intrusion response and incident management processes should be part of network design to provide a structured approach to addressing security incidents. Incident response plans define roles, responsibilities, and procedures for handling security breaches, minimizing their impact and facilitating recovery.

Redundancy and failover mechanisms are essential components of secure network design to ensure business continuity. High availability designs and failover systems help prevent disruptions caused by hardware failures or attacks.

Secure network design extends to the physical layer as well. Physical security measures, such as access controls, surveillance, and environmental controls, protect network infrastructure from unauthorized access or physical damage.

Secure configurations for network devices and systems are vital for reducing security risks. Hardening network devices, disabling unnecessary services, and regularly auditing configurations help eliminate potential vulnerabilities.

Secure coding practices should be employed when developing networked applications and services to prevent common vulnerabilities, such as SQL injection, cross-site scripting (XSS), and buffer overflows.

The concept of network resilience is essential in secure design. Resilience ensures that a network can withstand and recover from disruptions, whether caused by cyberattacks, natural disasters, or technical failures.

Security information and event management (SIEM) systems are valuable tools for collecting, correlating, and analyzing security event data from across the network. SIEM solutions provide insights into potential threats and support incident investigations.

Secure supply chain management is critical for verifying the security of hardware and software components before their integration into the network. Ensuring the integrity of components reduces the risk of compromised systems.

Secure remote access solutions, such as virtual private networks (VPNs) and secure remote desktops, enable authorized users to access network resources securely from remote locations.

To ensure secure network design, organizations must regularly conduct security assessments, vulnerability scans, and penetration testing to identify weaknesses and address them proactively.

In summary, network design principles for enhanced security are integral to protecting organizations' digital assets and data in an increasingly connected world. By implementing robust access controls, network segmentation, encryption, intrusion detection systems, and other security measures, organizations can create a secure network infrastructure that safeguards against a wide range of cyber threats and vulnerabilities. Security should be an integral part of network design from the outset, rather than an afterthought, to ensure the resilience and reliability of the network in the face of evolving threats.

Implementing defense in depth strategies is a fundamental approach to network security that involves the deployment of multiple layers of security controls to protect against a wide range of threats. This comprehensive strategy recognizes that no single security measure can provide absolute protection and instead relies on a combination of proactive and reactive measures.

At its core, defense in depth seeks to create multiple barriers and hurdles for potential attackers, making it more challenging for them to breach an organization's defenses and achieve their objectives. The strategy encompasses a wide range of security components, including technical, organizational, and human factors.

One of the foundational technical components of defense in depth is the implementation of firewalls at various points in the network architecture. Firewalls serve as gatekeepers, inspecting incoming and outgoing traffic, and enforcing access control policies to block or allow traffic based on predefined rules.

Network segmentation is another critical technical aspect of defense in depth. By dividing a network into smaller, isolated segments, organizations can limit the lateral movement of attackers within their infrastructure. This segmentation helps contain breaches and minimizes the potential damage.

Intrusion detection and prevention systems (IDPS) are key components that continuously monitor network traffic for signs of suspicious or malicious activity. IDPS solutions can identify patterns indicative of attacks and take action to block or alert on such activities.

Implementing strong access controls is essential to defense in depth. This includes authentication mechanisms, such as multi-factor authentication (MFA), to verify the identities of users and systems before granting access. Authorization processes ensure that users have appropriate permissions based on their roles and responsibilities.

Encryption plays a vital role in defense in depth by securing data both in transit and at rest. Encryption protocols, such as Transport Layer Security (TLS) and IPsec, protect data as it travels across networks or is stored on devices or servers.

Regular patch management is crucial for mitigating known vulnerabilities. Organizations should have processes in place to identify and apply patches and updates to software and hardware components promptly.

Security information and event management (SIEM) systems are valuable tools for collecting and analyzing security event data from across the network. SIEM solutions provide insights into potential threats, facilitate incident investigations, and support compliance efforts.

Antivirus and anti-malware solutions are essential for detecting and removing malicious software from systems.

These solutions scan files and programs for known malware signatures and behavior patterns.

Security awareness training is a key element of defense in depth that focuses on the human factor. Educating employees about security best practices, phishing awareness, and social engineering tactics empowers them to recognize and respond to potential threats effectively.

Incident response planning is an integral part of defense in depth. Organizations should develop detailed incident response plans that outline roles, responsibilities, and procedures for addressing security incidents. These plans help organizations respond quickly and minimize the impact of breaches.

Implementing network monitoring and log analysis tools allows organizations to identify abnormal behaviors or security incidents promptly. Continuous monitoring helps detect unauthorized access, suspicious activities, or signs of compromise.

Regular security assessments, including vulnerability scans and penetration testing, are essential for identifying weaknesses in the network infrastructure. These assessments provide insights into potential risks and vulnerabilities that require remediation.

Physical security measures should not be overlooked in defense in depth. Protecting network infrastructure, server rooms, and data centers from unauthorized access or physical damage is essential to overall security.

Secure supply chain management is crucial to ensure the integrity of hardware and software components before their integration into the network. Verifying the authenticity and security of components reduces the risk of compromised systems.

Intrusion response and containment measures should be well-defined and tested to isolate and mitigate security incidents effectively. Isolating compromised systems can prevent further damage and limit the attacker's access.

Security policies and procedures play a critical role in defense in depth. Organizations should have well-documented policies that define acceptable use, incident reporting, data handling, and security best practices.

Employee education and awareness programs should be ongoing efforts to keep personnel informed about emerging threats and security measures. Regular training and updates ensure that employees remain vigilant against evolving cyber threats.

Regularly updating and testing incident response plans ensures that the organization is well-prepared to respond to security incidents effectively. Conducting tabletop exercises and simulations can help personnel familiarize themselves with response procedures.

In summary, implementing defense in depth strategies is a multifaceted approach to network security that recognizes the complexity of the modern threat landscape. By deploying multiple layers of security controls, organizations can create a resilient defense posture that protects against a wide range of threats. This comprehensive strategy encompasses technical, organizational, and human elements to create a robust security framework that safeguards critical assets and data. Continuous monitoring, assessment, and education are essential components of maintaining an effective defense in depth strategy in the face of evolving cyber threats.

Chapter 3: Intrusion Detection and Prevention Systems

Intrusion Detection Systems (IDS) are integral components of modern cybersecurity, serving as vigilant guardians that monitor network and system activities for signs of unauthorized or malicious behavior. IDS plays a critical role in identifying security threats and enabling organizations to respond effectively to potential breaches.

An IDS operates by inspecting network traffic, system logs, and other data sources for suspicious patterns, anomalies, or known attack signatures. When an IDS detects activity that deviates from established norms or matches known attack patterns, it generates alerts or takes predefined actions to mitigate the threat.

There are two main categories of IDS: network-based intrusion detection systems (NIDS) and host-based intrusion detection systems (HIDS). NIDS are deployed at strategic points within a network, such as at the network perimeter or within critical segments, to monitor traffic passing through. HIDS, on the other hand, reside on individual host systems, such as servers or workstations, and monitor activities specific to those hosts.

NIDS are designed to detect network-level threats and attacks that target vulnerabilities in network protocols and services. They inspect traffic passing through the network, looking for patterns that match known attack signatures or behavior that deviates from established baselines. NIDS can identify threats like port scans, denial-of-service (DoS) attacks, and attempts to exploit known vulnerabilities.

HIDS, on the other hand, focus on host-specific activities and threats that may not be visible at the network level. They monitor system logs, file integrity, and system configurations for signs of compromise or unauthorized access. HIDS can detect activities such as unauthorized access attempts, changes to critical system files, or the presence of malware on a host.

One of the primary functions of an IDS is alerting. When the system detects suspicious or potentially malicious activity, it generates alerts to notify security personnel or administrators. These alerts typically include information about the detected event, such as the source IP address, destination IP address, timestamp, and a description of the activity.

The alerts generated by an IDS can vary in severity, ranging from low-level alerts that may indicate potential security risks to high-level alerts that signify a more immediate threat or intrusion. Security teams use the information provided in these alerts to assess the situation, investigate potential threats, and respond accordingly.

In addition to alerting, IDS can take other actions in response to detected threats. These actions can include blocking traffic from specific IP addresses, isolating compromised hosts from the network, or initiating incident response procedures. The actions taken by an IDS can be automated or manual, depending on the organization's security policies and the specific IDS configuration.

IDS can be further categorized based on their detection techniques. Signature-based detection relies on a database of known attack signatures and patterns to identify threats. This approach is effective at detecting known threats but may struggle with detecting new or previously unseen attacks.

Anomaly-based detection, on the other hand, focuses on identifying deviations from established baselines of normal behavior. It looks for unusual or unexpected patterns in network or host activities that may indicate an attack.

Anomaly-based detection is more effective at identifying novel threats but may also produce false positives.

Hybrid detection systems combine both signature-based and anomaly-based techniques to leverage the strengths of each approach. These systems use known attack signatures to detect known threats while also monitoring for deviations from baseline behavior to identify new and emerging threats.

The deployment of IDS should be carefully planned to ensure coverage of critical network segments and systems. Organizations typically position NIDS sensors at strategic points, such as network ingress and egress points, internal network segments, and within the demilitarized zone (DMZ). HIDS agents are installed on individual host systems where monitoring is required.

Tuning an IDS is an essential aspect of its effectiveness. This involves configuring the system to reduce false positives and false negatives. False positives occur when the IDS generates alerts for legitimate activities, while false negatives occur when it fails to detect actual threats. Balancing the detection sensitivity is crucial to ensure that the IDS provides meaningful alerts without overwhelming security teams with false alarms.

IDS should be kept up to date with the latest threat intelligence and attack signatures. Regular updates ensure that the IDS can identify new and evolving threats effectively. Organizations should also continuously monitor the performance and effectiveness of their IDS to adapt to changing threat landscapes.

Intrusion Detection Systems are valuable tools in the cybersecurity arsenal, helping organizations detect and respond to security threats in real-time. When properly configured and maintained, IDS can significantly enhance an organization's security posture, providing critical insights into potential threats and enabling swift incident response. Understanding the capabilities and limitations of IDS is essential for organizations seeking to protect their digital assets and data in an increasingly interconnected and threat-filled digital landscape.

Configuring an effective Intrusion Prevention System (IPS) is essential for safeguarding network security and preventing unauthorized access and attacks. An IPS serves as a critical security layer, inspecting network traffic, and taking proactive measures to block or mitigate potential threats in real-time.

The primary goal of an IPS is to identify and respond to malicious or suspicious activity within a network, including unauthorized access attempts, exploits, malware, and other security threats. Proper configuration of an IPS is essential to ensure it operates optimally and provides robust protection.

IPS can operate in two primary modes: in-line and out-of-band. In-line IPS devices are inserted directly into the network traffic path and have the ability to actively block or allow traffic based on predefined rules. Out-of-band IPS devices monitor traffic passively without directly affecting traffic flow but can provide alerts and recommendations for action.

Before configuring an IPS, it's essential to define a clear security policy that outlines the organization's security objectives, risk tolerance, and specific security requirements. This policy serves as a foundation for configuring the IPS to align with the organization's security goals.

One of the key aspects of configuring an IPS is creating and maintaining a rule set. Rule sets define the conditions under which the IPS should take action, such as blocking traffic, generating alerts, or allowing traffic to pass through. Rules should be based on known attack signatures, anomaly detection, or custom criteria tailored to the organization's needs.

IPS rules can be categorized into various groups, such as attack signatures, protocol anomalies, and custom rules. Attack signature rules are based on known patterns of malicious behavior, such as known malware signatures or attack patterns. Protocol anomaly rules focus on deviations from established network protocols, such as malformed packets or unusual protocol behavior. Custom rules allow organizations to define specific criteria for identifying threats or policy violations unique to their environment.

When configuring IPS rules, it's crucial to prioritize them to ensure that the most critical threats are addressed first. Prioritization ensures that high-severity threats are blocked or detected before lower-priority threats. Fine-tuning rule priorities helps avoid performance bottlenecks and ensures that the IPS operates efficiently.

Tuning an IPS is an ongoing process that involves adjusting rule settings to reduce false positives and false negatives. False positives occur when the IPS incorrectly identifies legitimate traffic as a threat, potentially blocking or alerting on harmless activities. False negatives occur when the IPS fails to detect actual threats. Balancing the sensitivity of the IPS is essential to minimize false alarms while maintaining effective threat detection.

Another important aspect of IPS configuration is defining actions to be taken when a rule is triggered. Actions can include blocking traffic, generating alerts, or logging information for further analysis. The choice of actions should align with the organization's security policy and response procedures.

To enhance the effectiveness of an IPS, organizations should keep it up to date with the latest threat intelligence and attack signatures. Regular updates ensure that the IPS can identify new and evolving threats effectively. Organizations should also have a process for testing and validating rule updates to minimize potential disruptions to network traffic.

Intrusion Prevention Systems can operate in different deployment modes, including in-line and out-of-band. In-line IPS devices are placed directly in the network traffic path and actively block or allow traffic based on predefined rules. In contrast, out-of-band IPS devices passively monitor traffic without directly impacting traffic flow.

To ensure redundancy and fault tolerance, organizations can deploy IPS devices in high availability configurations. High availability setups involve deploying multiple IPS devices in parallel, with one serving as the primary and the others as backups. If the primary device fails, the backup devices can seamlessly take over, ensuring continuous protection.

Continuous monitoring and analysis of IPS logs and alerts are essential to identify and respond to security incidents promptly. Security teams should regularly review IPS logs to investigate potential threats, track attack patterns, and refine rule sets based on emerging trends.

Integration with other security solutions, such as Security Information and Event Management (SIEM) systems, can enhance the effectiveness of an IPS. SIEM solutions can aggregate and correlate IPS alerts with other security events, providing a more comprehensive view of the organization's security posture.

Training and education for security personnel responsible for configuring and managing the IPS are crucial. Well-trained personnel can effectively interpret alerts, fine-tune rule sets, and respond to security incidents in a timely manner.

In summary, configuring an effective Intrusion Prevention System (IPS) is a critical component of a comprehensive cybersecurity strategy. An IPS serves as a proactive defense mechanism, monitoring network traffic for signs of malicious activity and taking action to protect the organization's assets. Proper configuration, rule management, sensitivity tuning, and integration with other security solutions are essential to ensure that the IPS operates optimally and provides robust protection against evolving threats in the digital landscape. Continuous monitoring, threat intelligence updates, and training are essential aspects of maintaining an effective IPS deployment that aligns with the organization's security goals and requirements.

Chapter 4: Next-Generation Firewall Technologies

Firewalls are fundamental components of modern security architectures, serving as the first line of defense against cyber threats and unauthorized access attempts. Their role in safeguarding networks and systems has evolved significantly to address the increasingly complex and dynamic threat landscape.

At its core, a firewall is a network security device or software application designed to monitor, filter, and control incoming and outgoing network traffic based on predetermined security rules. These rules, often referred to as firewall policies, dictate which traffic is allowed, blocked, or logged, depending on specific criteria.

The primary function of a firewall is to establish a barrier between a trusted internal network and untrusted external networks, such as the internet. By inspecting network packets and making decisions based on defined rules, firewalls help prevent unauthorized access to sensitive resources and protect against various cyber threats, including malware, hackers, and unauthorized data exfiltration.

Traditional firewalls operate primarily at the network layer (Layer 3) and transport layer (Layer 4) of the OSI model. These firewalls use a combination of static rules, such as IP addresses and port numbers, to determine whether network traffic should be allowed or denied. While effective for basic traffic filtering, traditional firewalls have limitations in dealing with more advanced threats and application-level attacks.

To address these limitations, modern firewalls have evolved to become Next-Generation Firewalls (NGFWs). NGFWs combine traditional firewall capabilities with additional features, such as application-layer filtering, intrusion detection and prevention (IDS/IPS), and deep packet inspection. This enhanced functionality enables NGFWs to provide more comprehensive security by inspecting and controlling traffic at the application layer (Layer 7) based on application and user identity.

Intrusion detection and prevention systems (IDS/IPS) are integral components of NGFWs, allowing them to identify and respond to known attack patterns and suspicious behavior. IDS monitors network traffic for signs of potential threats and generates alerts, while IPS takes proactive measures to block or mitigate threats based on predefined rules.

Application-layer filtering in NGFWs enables organizations to control the use of specific applications and services. This feature is crucial for enforcing security policies, restricting access to non-business-related applications, and preventing the spread of malware through malicious applications.

Deep packet inspection (DPI) is a key technology in NGFWs that allows for the thorough analysis of packet contents. DPI examines not only header information but also the payload of packets, enabling the detection of advanced threats, evasion techniques, and zero-day vulnerabilities.

Stateful inspection, another feature of modern firewalls, maintains the state of active connections and enforces security policies based on the stateful context of network traffic. This functionality ensures that only legitimate traffic associated with established connections is allowed through the firewall.

Firewalls can be deployed in various network architectures to meet specific security requirements. In a perimeter or network edge deployment, firewalls protect the boundary between an organization's internal network and the external world, filtering incoming and outgoing traffic to prevent unauthorized access and threats.

Internal firewalls, also known as internal segmentation firewalls (ISFWs), are positioned within an organization's internal network to segment and isolate specific network segments or departments. ISFWs enhance security by limiting lateral movement within the network and containing breaches to specific areas.

Virtual firewalls are designed for virtualized environments, such as cloud infrastructure and virtual data centers. These firewalls provide security for virtual machines (VMs) and containers, ensuring that traffic between virtualized workloads is protected.

Web application firewalls (WAFs) are specialized firewalls designed to protect web applications from attacks and vulnerabilities. WAFs inspect HTTP and HTTPS traffic, identifying and blocking malicious requests, SQL injection, cross-site scripting (XSS), and other application-level threats.

Cloud-based firewalls are hosted in the cloud and provide security for cloud-native applications and services. These firewalls are particularly relevant in multi-cloud and hybrid cloud environments, where traditional on-premises firewalls may not provide adequate protection.

Intrusion prevention system (IPS) appliances are standalone devices or software solutions that focus on the detection and prevention of network-based attacks. IPS solutions monitor network traffic for known attack patterns and take proactive measures to block or mitigate threats.

Unified Threat Management (UTM) appliances combine multiple security functions into a single device, including firewall, antivirus, intrusion detection and prevention, content filtering, and VPN capabilities. UTM appliances offer comprehensive security for small to medium-sized businesses (SMBs) and remote offices.

When configuring firewalls, organizations must define firewall policies that align with their security objectives and risk tolerance. Firewall policies specify the rules for allowing or blocking traffic based on source and destination addresses, port numbers, and application-level criteria.

Firewall rules can be configured to allow specific traffic, block specific traffic, or log specific events. Fine-tuning firewall policies is crucial to minimize false positives (blocking legitimate traffic) and false negatives (allowing malicious traffic). Regularly reviewing and updating firewall rules is essential to adapt to changing security requirements and emerging threats. Organizations should conduct periodic firewall rule audits to ensure that policies remain effective and aligned with security policies. Firewalls play a critical role in securing network communications and protecting against a wide range of threats. Their evolution into Next-Generation Firewalls (NGFWs) has enabled them to provide more comprehensive security by inspecting traffic at the application layer and incorporating features like IDS/IPS, deep packet inspection, and application-level filtering. As organizations continue to face evolving cyber threats, firewalls remain a vital component of modern security strategies, helping safeguard networks and data from unauthorized access and malicious activity. Configuring firewalls to provide advanced security measures is crucial in today's complex and evolving threat landscape. Advanced firewall configuration goes beyond the basics of allowing or blocking traffic, delving into the fine-tuned controls and policies that ensure robust protection for networks and systems.

One aspect of advanced firewall configuration is the creation of custom rules tailored to an organization's specific security requirements. Custom rules allow organizations to define precise criteria for traffic handling, enabling them to address unique security challenges effectively.

Custom rules can be based on a variety of factors, including source and destination IP addresses, port numbers, application types, and user identities. These rules empower organizations to enforce security policies that align with their business goals and risk tolerance.

Intrusion Detection and Prevention Systems (IDS/IPS) integration is a critical component of advanced firewall configuration. IDS/IPS functionality enhances a firewall's threat detection and response capabilities by identifying known attack patterns and suspicious behavior within network traffic.

By integrating IDS/IPS with a firewall, organizations can benefit from real-time threat intelligence and automated actions that proactively block or mitigate security threats. This synergy between firewall and IDS/IPS provides a more robust defense against emerging threats.

Another advanced firewall configuration technique is the implementation of application-layer filtering rules. Unlike traditional firewalls that operate at the network and transport layers, advanced firewalls can inspect and control traffic at the application layer (Layer 7) based on application and user identity.

Application-layer filtering rules allow organizations to control the use of specific applications and services. This capability is essential for enforcing security policies, restricting access to non-business-related applications, and preventing the spread of malware through malicious applications.

Deep Packet Inspection (DPI) is a technology integral to advanced firewall configuration. DPI enables firewalls to inspect the contents of network packets at a granular level, including the payload of packets. This in-depth analysis provides insights into the actual data being transmitted, allowing firewalls to detect advanced threats, evasion techniques, and zero-day vulnerabilities.

By examining packet payloads, DPI can identify patterns indicative of malware, malicious payloads, or unauthorized data transfers. This level of inspection helps organizations stay ahead of sophisticated attackers and respond effectively to emerging threats.

Stateful Inspection, a foundational feature of advanced firewalls, maintains the state of active connections and enforces security policies based on the context of network traffic. Stateful inspection ensures that only legitimate traffic associated with established connections is allowed through the firewall.

The stateful context includes information such as source and destination IP addresses, port numbers, and connection status. By considering the state of each connection, advanced firewalls can accurately evaluate traffic and make informed decisions based on security policies.

Network Address Translation (NAT) is another advanced firewall feature commonly used to manage IP addresses and enhance security. NAT allows organizations to map private internal IP addresses to a single public-facing IP address, providing a level of anonymity and security for internal systems.

NAT also aids in conserving IPv4 addresses, which are limited in availability, by allowing multiple internal devices to share a single public IP address. This obfuscation of internal network structure enhances security by making it more challenging for external entities to identify and target specific internal devices.

Intrusion Response and Evasion Mitigation techniques are vital components of advanced firewall configurations. These techniques involve proactive measures to detect and respond to advanced threats and evasion attempts.

Firewalls equipped with intrusion response capabilities can take actions such as blocking or rate-limiting traffic from suspicious IP addresses, dynamically adjusting security policies, and initiating incident response procedures. These actions help organizations minimize the impact of security incidents and protect critical assets.

Evasion mitigation focuses on countering techniques employed by attackers to evade detection by traditional security measures. Advanced firewalls can detect and thwart evasion attempts, ensuring that threats are not overlooked due to obfuscation or evasion techniques.

Policy-based Routing is an advanced firewall feature that allows organizations to route traffic based on specific policies or criteria. This functionality can be valuable for optimizing network performance and ensuring that critical traffic follows preferred paths.

Organizations can create policies that dictate how traffic should be routed based on factors like source and destination addresses, application types, or security requirements. Policy-based routing enhances control over network traffic and enables organizations to meet specific operational or security objectives.

Firewalls with Threat Intelligence Integration capabilities leverage external threat intelligence feeds to enhance threat detection and response. These feeds provide up-to-date information about known threats, indicators of compromise (IoCs), and emerging attack patterns.

By integrating threat intelligence into firewall configurations, organizations can enrich their security posture and proactively block traffic associated with known threats. This integration strengthens security by aligning firewall rules with real-time threat intelligence.

Dynamic Application Control (DAC) is a feature in advanced firewalls that allows organizations to control applications and services dynamically based on their characteristics and risk profiles. DAC enhances security by adapting to changing application landscapes and threat environments.

DAC categorizes applications based on factors like risk level, reputation, and business relevance. Organizations can then apply policies to allow, block, or restrict the use of specific applications, ensuring that security policies align with evolving business needs.

Multi-Factor Authentication (MFA) Integration is an advanced firewall capability that enhances security by requiring multiple authentication factors for remote access. MFA adds an extra layer of security beyond traditional username and password authentication.

By integrating MFA with firewalls, organizations can ensure that remote users must provide additional authentication factors, such as tokens or biometrics, to establish a secure connection. This reduces the risk of unauthorized access and strengthens security for remote access scenarios.

In summary, advanced firewall configuration and policies are critical components of modern cybersecurity strategies. These configurations empower organizations to tailor their security measures to align with their specific business goals and risk tolerance. By implementing advanced features such as IDS/IPS integration, application-layer filtering, DPI, NAT, intrusion response, and threat intelligence integration, organizations can create a robust defense against the evolving threat landscape. Advanced firewalls play a pivotal role in safeguarding networks, data, and systems from an array of security threats while providing the flexibility and agility needed to adapt to changing business needs and emerging threats.

Chapter 5: Advanced Threat Intelligence and Analysis

Leveraging threat intelligence sources is a fundamental aspect of modern cybersecurity, enabling organizations to enhance their defenses and stay ahead of evolving threats. Threat intelligence provides valuable insights into the tactics, techniques, and procedures (TTPs) employed by threat actors, helping organizations proactively identify and mitigate security risks.

One of the primary benefits of threat intelligence is its ability to provide organizations with a contextual understanding of the threat landscape. This understanding includes information about current and emerging threats, vulnerabilities, and attack patterns relevant to the organization's industry, geographic location, and technology stack.

Threat intelligence sources encompass a wide range of repositories and providers, each offering unique insights into the threat landscape. These sources can be categorized into several key categories, including open-source intelligence (OSINT), commercial intelligence providers, government agencies, information sharing and analysis centers (ISACs), and internal sources.

Open-source intelligence (OSINT) refers to publicly available information that can be accessed by anyone. OSINT sources include websites, forums, social media platforms, and other publicly accessible data repositories. Security researchers and analysts often leverage OSINT to gather information about known threats, vulnerabilities, and malicious actors.

Commercial intelligence providers offer subscription-based services that deliver curated threat intelligence feeds, reports, and analysis to organizations. These providers collect and analyze data from various sources, including their own research, open-source data, and dark web monitoring. Commercial intelligence services provide organizations with up-to-date threat information and actionable insights.

Government agencies, such as the United States' Cybersecurity and Infrastructure Security Agency (CISA) and the United Kingdom's National Cyber Security Centre (NCSC), publish threat intelligence reports and advisories. These reports often include information about known vulnerabilities, indicators of compromise (IoCs), and recommended mitigation strategies. Government agencies are valuable sources of authoritative threat intelligence.

Information Sharing and Analysis Centers (ISACs) are industry-specific organizations that facilitate the sharing of cybersecurity threat intelligence among member organizations. ISACs provide a platform for companies within a particular industry to collaborate on threat information sharing and receive sector-specific threat intelligence.

Internal sources of threat intelligence originate from an organization's own security infrastructure, logs, and incident response activities. These internal sources provide insights into the organization's specific threat landscape, including ongoing attacks, vulnerabilities, and trends affecting its environment.

To effectively leverage threat intelligence sources, organizations should establish a structured process for collecting, analyzing, and applying threat intelligence. This process includes several key steps:

Data Collection: Organizations should identify relevant threat intelligence sources and collect data from these sources. This data may include indicators of compromise (IoCs), threat actor profiles, malware signatures, and vulnerability information.

Data Normalization: Threat intelligence data often comes in various formats and structures. Normalizing the data involves standardizing it into a common format for analysis and integration with existing security tools and systems.

Analysis and Enrichment: Security analysts and researchers analyze the collected threat intelligence to identify patterns, trends, and potential risks. Enrichment involves augmenting the data with additional context, such as geolocation information, known attack techniques, and attribution details.

Correlation and Prioritization: Threat intelligence data should be correlated with an organization's existing security data, such as logs and network traffic. Correlation helps identify potential threats and vulnerabilities that align with the organization's assets and infrastructure. Prioritization involves ranking threats based on their severity and relevance to the organization.

Integration with Security Tools: Threat intelligence should be integrated with security tools and technologies, such as intrusion detection systems (IDS), security information and event management (SIEM) systems, and firewalls. This integration enables automated threat detection, alerting, and response based on threat intelligence feeds.

Incident Response and Mitigation: When a threat is identified through threat intelligence, organizations should have incident response plans in place to quickly mitigate the threat. This may involve isolating affected systems, applying security patches, or blocking malicious traffic.

Continuous Monitoring and Updating: Threat intelligence is dynamic, and the threat landscape evolves constantly. Organizations must continuously monitor threat intelligence sources, update their security policies and controls, and adapt their defenses to address emerging threats.

Threat intelligence sharing and collaboration within the cybersecurity community are essential for collective defense against cyber threats. Organizations can participate in threat sharing platforms and forums to contribute and receive threat intelligence from peer organizations, industry groups, and government agencies.

Many organizations also use threat intelligence platforms (TIPs) to streamline the collection, analysis, and dissemination of threat intelligence. TIPs provide a centralized repository for threat data, automate data processing tasks, and facilitate information sharing and collaboration.

In addition to proactive threat intelligence, organizations can benefit from retrospective analysis of past incidents and breaches. This retrospective threat intelligence helps organizations understand how previous attacks occurred, the tactics used by threat actors, and the vulnerabilities that were exploited. This knowledge can inform future security strategies and help organizations better defend against similar threats.

Overall, leveraging threat intelligence sources is a critical component of a comprehensive cybersecurity strategy. Threat intelligence provides organizations with valuable insights into the threat landscape, allowing them to identify and respond to security risks proactively. By establishing structured processes for collecting, analyzing, and applying threat intelligence, organizations can enhance their security posture and protect their assets and data from evolving cyber threats. Collaboration and information sharing within the cybersecurity community further strengthen collective defenses and contribute to a safer digital environment.

Analyzing and mitigating advanced threats is a critical imperative in today's ever-evolving cybersecurity landscape, where cybercriminals constantly refine their tactics, techniques, and procedures (TTPs) to breach defenses and exploit vulnerabilities.

Advanced threats encompass a wide spectrum of sophisticated attacks designed to evade traditional security measures and inflict significant damage on organizations. These threats may include advanced persistent threats (APTs), zero-day exploits, ransomware attacks, and nation-state-sponsored campaigns.

One of the key challenges in analyzing and mitigating advanced threats is their ability to remain stealthy and evade detection for extended periods. Advanced threats often employ various evasion techniques, such as polymorphic malware, rootkit-based attacks, and fileless malware, to avoid triggering alarms in traditional security systems.

To effectively analyze advanced threats, organizations must deploy advanced threat detection solutions capable of identifying anomalous behavior and detecting unknown or zero-day threats. These solutions leverage machine learning, behavioral analytics, and threat intelligence to identify deviations from normal network and system behavior that may indicate the presence of an advanced threat.

Behavioral analysis focuses on understanding how systems, applications, and users typically behave within an organization's network. By establishing a baseline of normal behavior, security systems can detect deviations, which may indicate suspicious or malicious activity.

Machine learning algorithms play a crucial role in identifying advanced threats by continuously analyzing vast amounts of data to uncover patterns and anomalies. Machine learning models can detect unusual network traffic, unrecognized files, and suspicious user behaviors, even if these activities do not match known attack signatures.

Threat intelligence is another essential component of advanced threat analysis. Threat intelligence feeds provide organizations with up-to-date information about known threats, indicators of compromise (IoCs), and emerging attack patterns. This information is invaluable for identifying and responding to advanced threats effectively.

Once an advanced threat is detected, organizations must initiate an incident response plan to mitigate the impact and prevent further damage. Incident response involves a coordinated effort to contain, eradicate, and recover from the threat while preserving evidence for analysis and legal purposes.

Containment measures may include isolating affected systems from the network, disabling compromised accounts, or implementing network segmentation to prevent lateral movement by threat actors. Eradication involves removing all traces of the threat from affected systems, including malware removal, patching vulnerabilities, and restoring affected services to normal operation.

Forensic analysis plays a crucial role in understanding the scope and impact of an advanced threat. Forensic investigators gather evidence from affected systems, logs, and network traffic to reconstruct the attack timeline, identify the threat actor's tactics, and determine the extent of data breaches.

Advanced threat mitigation often involves the application of zero-trust principles, where organizations operate on the assumption that no system or user can be fully trusted, and strict access controls are enforced. Implementing least privilege access, micro-segmentation, and continuous monitoring are key elements of a zero-trust security model.

Threat hunting is a proactive approach to identifying and mitigating advanced threats before they cause significant harm. Threat hunters are security experts who actively seek out signs of advanced threats within an organization's environment, using a combination of tools, data analysis, and expertise to uncover hidden threats.

Security information and event management (SIEM) systems play a critical role in advanced threat analysis by collecting and correlating data from various sources, such as logs, network traffic, and security alerts. SIEM systems provide a centralized platform for real-time monitoring and analysis, enabling security teams to identify and respond to threats promptly.

Continuous monitoring and security analytics are essential for detecting advanced threats that may evolve and change tactics over time. By analyzing large volumes of data and applying advanced analytics techniques, organizations can identify subtle patterns indicative of advanced threats.

Endpoint detection and response (EDR) solutions are designed to monitor and protect individual endpoints, such as laptops, desktops, and servers, from advanced threats. EDR solutions offer real-time visibility into endpoint activity, allowing security teams to detect and respond to threats at the endpoint level.

Cloud-based security solutions have become increasingly important for mitigating advanced threats in cloud environments. These solutions offer threat detection and response capabilities tailored to cloud workloads and services, helping organizations secure their cloud assets effectively.

Advanced threat intelligence sharing and collaboration among organizations and industry groups can enhance collective defenses. Sharing threat intelligence about advanced threats, indicators of compromise, and attack techniques helps organizations stay informed and respond more effectively to emerging threats.

Employee training and awareness programs are essential for mitigating advanced threats that often target human vulnerabilities, such as social engineering attacks. Educating employees about the risks and tactics used by threat actors can help prevent successful attacks.

In summary, analyzing and mitigating advanced threats require a multi-faceted approach that combines advanced threat detection, incident response, containment, forensic analysis, and continuous monitoring. Organizations must deploy sophisticated security solutions, leverage threat intelligence, and adopt a zero-trust security model to protect against advanced threats effectively. Proactive threat hunting, SIEM systems, EDR solutions, and cloud security measures are vital components of a comprehensive defense strategy. Collaboration and information sharing within the cybersecurity community further strengthen collective defenses and contribute to a safer digital environment in the face of relentless and evolving advanced threats.

Chapter 6: Cloud Security and Virtualization

Cloud security best practices are essential for organizations transitioning to cloud environments to protect their data, applications, and infrastructure effectively.

One fundamental aspect of cloud security is understanding the shared responsibility model, where cloud providers are responsible for the security of the cloud infrastructure, while customers are responsible for securing their data and applications within that infrastructure.

Implementing robust access controls is crucial in cloud security, as it ensures that only authorized users can access cloud resources and data. Utilizing identity and access management (IAM) solutions is an effective way to manage user identities, roles, and permissions.

Multi-factor authentication (MFA) adds an extra layer of security by requiring users to provide multiple forms of verification before gaining access, reducing the risk of unauthorized access even if login credentials are compromised.

Encrypting data both in transit and at rest is a critical cloud security practice. This ensures that data remains confidential and secure, even if intercepted or accessed by unauthorized parties.

Data loss prevention (DLP) solutions help organizations identify and prevent the unauthorized sharing or exposure of sensitive data within their cloud environments, mitigating the risk of data breaches.

Regularly auditing and monitoring cloud environments is essential for detecting and responding to security incidents. Cloud-native monitoring tools and security information and event management (SIEM) solutions can provide insights into suspicious activities.

Implementing network segmentation within cloud environments can isolate sensitive workloads and applications, reducing the potential blast radius in case of a security breach.

Maintaining up-to-date backups of cloud data is crucial for disaster recovery and business continuity. Organizations should regularly test their backup and recovery processes to ensure data can be restored effectively.

Patch management for cloud resources is essential to address known vulnerabilities and security patches promptly. Automated patch management solutions can streamline this process.

Container security is critical for organizations using containerization technologies in the cloud. Implementing security scanning and best practices for container image management helps prevent vulnerabilities in containerized applications.

Cloud providers offer a wide range of security services and tools that organizations can leverage to enhance their cloud security posture. These services may include managed firewalls, intrusion detection systems (IDS), and security information and event management (SIEM) solutions.

Regular security training and awareness programs for employees help educate them about cloud security risks, best practices, and how to recognize and respond to phishing and social engineering attempts.

Creating an incident response plan specific to cloud security incidents ensures that organizations can respond quickly and effectively to security breaches or incidents within their cloud environments.

Third-party security assessments and penetration testing can help organizations identify vulnerabilities and weaknesses in their cloud infrastructure and applications that may not be apparent through internal testing.

Compliance with regulatory requirements, such as GDPR, HIPAA, or PCI DSS, is critical for organizations that store or process sensitive data in the cloud. Ensuring that cloud deployments align with these requirements is essential to avoid regulatory penalties.

Continuous security monitoring and automated remediation processes help organizations stay vigilant against emerging threats and respond quickly to security incidents.

Implementing a secure DevOps (DevSecOps) culture in cloud environments ensures that security is integrated into the development and deployment processes, reducing security risks associated with rapid development cycles.

Regularly reviewing and updating cloud security policies and procedures is essential to adapt to evolving threats and changes in cloud environments.

Engaging with a cloud security provider or consulting firm with expertise in cloud security can help organizations assess their cloud security posture and implement best practices effectively.

Cloud security best practices are an ongoing effort, requiring organizations to stay informed about the latest threats and security technologies to protect their cloud assets effectively.

In summary, cloud security best practices are essential for organizations to protect their data, applications, and infrastructure in cloud environments. Understanding the shared responsibility model, implementing robust access controls, encryption, and DLP, regularly auditing and monitoring cloud environments, and maintaining backups are fundamental steps. Leveraging cloud provider security services, conducting security training, and complying with regulations are also critical. Implementing a secure DevOps culture and engaging with cloud security experts contribute to a comprehensive and effective cloud security strategy. Organizations must remain vigilant, adapting to evolving threats and technologies to secure their cloud assets continually.

Virtualization security considerations are paramount in today's technology landscape, as organizations increasingly adopt virtualization technologies to optimize resource utilization, enhance scalability, and reduce hardware costs.
Virtualization, which involves creating virtual instances of operating systems and applications on a single physical server, introduces a unique set of security challenges that organizations must address to ensure the confidentiality, integrity, and availability of their data and applications.
One key consideration in virtualization security is the shared resource model, where multiple virtual machines (VMs) share the same underlying physical hardware. While this sharing of resources is cost-effective and efficient, it also introduces the potential for security breaches if not properly segmented and isolated.
Organizations must implement strong isolation mechanisms to prevent one VM from accessing or affecting the resources of another VM. This includes using features like hypervisor-based security controls and network segmentation to ensure VMs operate in separate and secure environments.
Hypervisor security is a critical aspect of virtualization security, as the hypervisor is responsible for managing and controlling VMs. Securing the hypervisor involves maintaining its integrity, applying security patches promptly, and restricting unauthorized access.
One way to enhance hypervisor security is through hardware-assisted virtualization, which leverages features

provided by modern processors to isolate VMs more effectively and reduce the attack surface.

VM escape vulnerabilities, where an attacker exploits a flaw in a VM to break out and access the host system or other VMs, are a significant concern. Organizations must keep their hypervisors and VMs updated with security patches to mitigate these risks.

Secure boot and measured boot are technologies that ensure the integrity of the hypervisor and VMs during the boot process, preventing unauthorized modifications or malware infections.

Another virtualization security consideration is the management plane, where administrators control and configure VMs. Securing the management plane involves implementing strong authentication, access controls, and encryption to protect sensitive administrative data and actions.

Virtual machine sprawl, where numerous VMs are created but not properly managed or monitored, can lead to security vulnerabilities. Organizations should have policies and processes in place to identify and decommission unnecessary or unused VMs.

Security groups and role-based access controls (RBAC) are essential tools for managing and restricting administrative access to VMs and the virtualization infrastructure. Only authorized personnel should have access to virtualization management interfaces.

Virtual machine image integrity is crucial to ensure that VMs are not compromised by malicious or tampered images. Organizations should maintain a secure image repository, validate image integrity, and use trusted sources for VM images.

Virtualization security extends to the network, where organizations must consider how VMs communicate and access external resources. Network security controls, such as firewalls, intrusion detection and prevention systems (IDS/IPS), and network segmentation, help protect VMs from external threats.

Implementing network segmentation within the virtualized environment isolates VMs into separate network segments, reducing the lateral movement of threats in case of a security breach.

Intrusion detection and prevention systems (IDS/IPS) specifically designed for virtualized environments can help monitor VM traffic and detect malicious activity or unauthorized access.

Virtual private networks (VPNs) or secure tunnels can be used to encrypt communication between VMs or between VMs and external networks, ensuring data confidentiality and integrity.

Storage security in virtualized environments is critical to protect data at rest. Organizations should encrypt virtual machine disks and implement access controls to prevent unauthorized access to storage resources.

Backup and disaster recovery strategies for VMs are essential to ensure data availability and business continuity. Regularly testing backups and recovery procedures is crucial to verify their effectiveness.

Automation and orchestration tools can help streamline security management tasks in virtualized environments, ensuring consistent and compliant configurations across VMs and hosts.

Compliance with industry standards and regulations, such as the Payment Card Industry Data Security Standard (PCI DSS) or the Health Insurance Portability and Accountability Act (HIPAA), is essential for organizations handling sensitive data within virtualized environments.

Security audits and assessments should be conducted regularly to identify vulnerabilities and ensure compliance with security policies and best practices.

Virtualization security should also address the protection of virtualization management interfaces and the hypervisor itself from insider threats. Insider threats may include malicious or compromised administrators who have access to critical systems.

Security monitoring and logging are essential for detecting and investigating security incidents within virtualized environments. Organizations should collect and analyze logs from VMs, hypervisors, and virtualization management systems to identify abnormal activities.

Intrusion detection and response mechanisms should be in place to respond to security incidents promptly. This may include isolating compromised VMs, collecting forensic evidence, and implementing corrective actions.

In summary, virtualization security considerations are integral to maintaining the security and integrity of virtualized environments. Organizations must address shared resource risks, secure the hypervisor, manage VM sprawl, control administrative access, protect image integrity, and implement network and storage security measures. Compliance, automation, and monitoring are essential components of a robust virtualization security strategy. By implementing these measures, organizations can harness the benefits of virtualization while minimizing security risks and ensuring the confidentiality, integrity, and availability of their data and applications.

Chapter 7: Secure Mobile Device Management

Mobile device security policies and compliance are crucial components of a comprehensive cybersecurity strategy in today's mobile-centric world, where smartphones, tablets, and other mobile devices play a significant role in both personal and professional life.

Organizations must recognize the importance of mobile device security policies, as mobile devices have become integral tools for employees to access corporate networks, applications, and sensitive data remotely. The proliferation of mobile devices presents unique security challenges, as these devices are inherently more vulnerable to loss, theft, and unauthorized access compared to traditional desktop or laptop computers.

A mobile device security policy is a set of guidelines and procedures that govern the secure use, management, and protection of mobile devices within an organization. Such policies are designed to mitigate security risks associated with mobile devices and ensure compliance with industry regulations and best practices.

One fundamental aspect of mobile device security policy development is defining the scope of the policy, which includes specifying the types of mobile devices covered, such as smartphones, tablets, laptops, and wearables, and the operating systems and platforms they use.

Mobile device management (MDM) and mobile application management (MAM) solutions play a crucial role in enforcing mobile device security policies. These solutions provide organizations with the ability to remotely manage and configure mobile devices, enforce security settings, and ensure compliance with policy requirements.

Authentication and access control are critical elements of mobile device security. Organizations should require strong, multi-factor authentication for device access, application access, and data access to prevent unauthorized use of mobile devices.

Encryption is essential for protecting data on mobile devices, both at rest and in transit. Mobile device security policies should mandate encryption of sensitive data stored on devices and during data transmission. This includes data stored within mobile apps, email communications, and data backups.

Device configuration and patch management are vital for maintaining the security of mobile devices. Organizations should enforce policies that require regular software updates and patches to address vulnerabilities and security weaknesses in the device's operating system and applications.

Mobile app security is a significant concern, as malicious or poorly designed apps can pose a risk to the security and privacy of mobile device users. Organizations should establish policies for app installation and review, ensuring that only trusted and approved apps are allowed on corporate devices.

Remote wipe and data loss prevention (DLP) capabilities are essential for mitigating the risks associated with lost or stolen devices. Mobile device security policies should outline procedures for remote wiping of corporate data from lost or compromised devices to prevent unauthorized access.

Mobile device security policies should also address the use of public Wi-Fi networks, as these networks are often less secure and can expose mobile devices to various security threats. Policies may include guidelines on VPN usage, secure Wi-Fi configurations, and the risks associated with connecting to untrusted networks.

User training and awareness are critical components of mobile device security policies. Organizations should provide employees with education and guidance on mobile device security best practices, including safe browsing habits, password management, and recognizing phishing attempts.

Compliance with industry-specific regulations, such as the General Data Protection Regulation (GDPR) or the Health Insurance Portability and Accountability Act (HIPAA), is a key consideration for organizations that handle sensitive data on mobile devices. Mobile device security policies should align with regulatory requirements to ensure legal compliance.

Regular security assessments and audits are essential for evaluating the effectiveness of mobile device security policies and compliance. Organizations should conduct vulnerability assessments, penetration testing, and mobile device security audits to identify weaknesses and areas for improvement.

Incident response and reporting procedures should be clearly defined in mobile device security policies. Employees should know how to report lost or stolen devices, security incidents, or suspected breaches promptly.

The use of personal mobile devices for work, often referred to as bring your own device (BYOD) policies, requires careful consideration within mobile device security policies. BYOD policies should specify security requirements for personal devices used for work purposes, including app whitelisting, data separation, and remote management.

Cloud-based mobile device management (MDM) and mobile application management (MAM) solutions offer organizations flexibility in managing and securing mobile devices across various platforms and operating systems. These solutions can enforce policies, remotely configure devices, and provide real-time visibility into device security.

Audit trails and logs of mobile device activities should be maintained to track user actions, detect security incidents, and support forensic investigations if necessary. Policies should specify retention periods for logs and data, as well as access controls for sensitive logs.

Regular security training and awareness programs for employees help educate them about mobile device security risks and best practices. Employees should understand the importance of safeguarding their devices, using strong authentication methods, and adhering to mobile device security policies.

In summary, mobile device security policies and compliance are essential for organizations to protect sensitive data, maintain regulatory compliance, and mitigate security risks associated with mobile devices. These policies should encompass various aspects, including authentication, encryption, device management, app security, remote wipe capabilities, and user education. Regular assessments and audits ensure policy effectiveness, and incident response procedures help organizations respond promptly to security incidents. Cloud-based MDM and MAM solutions provide flexibility in managing and securing mobile devices, while BYOD policies address the challenges of personal device usage in the workplace. Ultimately, a well-defined and comprehensive mobile device security policy is crucial to safeguarding organizational assets in an increasingly mobile-driven world.

Implementing secure mobile device management (MDM) solutions is a critical step for organizations seeking to protect their data, applications, and networks in the face of increasing mobile device usage.

Mobile devices, such as smartphones and tablets, have become indispensable tools for both personal and professional use, and their ubiquity has made them a prime target for cyberattacks and data breaches.

Mobile device management solutions are comprehensive platforms that allow organizations to control, secure, and manage mobile devices, ensuring that they comply with corporate security policies and standards.

The first step in implementing secure MDM solutions is to assess the organization's mobile device landscape, identifying the types of devices in use, the operating systems they run, and the security risks associated with each.

This assessment should consider whether the organization provides corporate-owned devices, allows for bring your own device (BYOD) policies, or operates in a hybrid environment that includes both corporate and personal devices.

Once the mobile device landscape is understood, organizations can select the appropriate MDM solution that aligns with their needs, whether it's an on-premises solution, a cloud-based solution, or a combination of both.

The next crucial step is device enrollment, where devices are registered with the MDM solution. Enrollment typically involves users downloading an MDM app or profile onto their devices and then authenticating themselves to link the device with the organization's MDM system.

Strong authentication methods, such as multi-factor authentication (MFA), should be used during the enrollment process to ensure that only authorized users can access and manage their devices.

After enrollment, organizations can establish security policies and configurations for mobile devices. These policies can include requirements for passcodes or biometric authentication, encryption settings, and restrictions on certain device features or applications.

Organizations should also define acceptable use policies that guide employees on the appropriate use of mobile devices, including how to handle sensitive data and access corporate resources securely.

Device inventory and asset management are critical components of secure MDM solutions. Organizations should maintain an up-to-date inventory of all managed devices, including their hardware and software specifications, to track their status and compliance with security policies.

Mobile device management solutions offer remote management capabilities, allowing organizations to perform tasks like remotely locking or wiping lost or stolen devices, updating device configurations, and pushing software updates and patches.

Regularly monitoring and auditing mobile devices for security compliance is essential. Continuous monitoring ensures that devices remain compliant with security policies, and organizations can promptly detect and address any violations or anomalies.

Mobile application management (MAM) is an integral part of MDM solutions, allowing organizations to control and secure mobile apps. MAM capabilities include app whitelisting, blacklisting, and app distribution to ensure that only authorized and secure apps are used on corporate devices.

Secure content management is another important aspect of MDM solutions, enabling organizations to protect sensitive data on mobile devices. This may involve encryption of data at rest and in transit, secure document sharing, and data loss prevention (DLP) measures.

Security analytics and reporting provide organizations with insights into the security posture of their mobile device fleet. By analyzing data and generating reports, organizations can identify trends, vulnerabilities, and areas for improvement in their mobile security strategy.

Integration with other security solutions, such as security information and event management (SIEM) systems and identity and access management (IAM) solutions, enhances the overall security ecosystem and allows for centralized security monitoring and enforcement.

User education and awareness programs are crucial for ensuring that employees understand the importance of mobile device security and adhere to security policies. Training should cover topics like safe app installation, recognizing phishing attempts, and reporting lost or stolen devices promptly. Compliance with industry regulations and standards, such as the General Data Protection Regulation (GDPR) or the Health Insurance Portability and Accountability Act (HIPAA), is essential for organizations handling sensitive data on mobile devices. MDM solutions should align with these regulations to avoid legal and financial consequences.

Implementing a secure mobile device management solution is an ongoing process that requires regular updates and adjustments to address evolving threats and technologies.

Organizations should stay informed about emerging mobile security threats, vulnerabilities, and best practices to adapt their MDM strategies accordingly.

Furthermore, organizations should conduct periodic security assessments and audits to evaluate the effectiveness of their MDM solution and identify areas for improvement.

Mobile security is a dynamic field, and organizations must be proactive in their approach to secure mobile device management to protect against constantly evolving threats.

In summary, implementing secure mobile device management solutions is imperative for organizations to safeguard their data, applications, and networks in an increasingly mobile-driven world. It involves assessing the mobile device landscape, selecting the right MDM solution, enrolling devices securely, establishing policies and configurations, and maintaining compliance. Regular monitoring, user education, and integration with other security solutions enhance the overall security posture. Adaptation to emerging threats and continuous improvement are essential for a robust mobile device security strategy that can withstand evolving challenges in the mobile security landscape.

Chapter 8: Network Segmentation and Micro-Segmentation

Network segmentation strategies are essential components of a comprehensive cybersecurity approach, designed to enhance security by dividing a network into smaller, isolated segments or zones.

These segments, often referred to as subnetworks or VLANs (Virtual Local Area Networks), allow organizations to compartmentalize their network infrastructure, creating separate zones with controlled access and security policies.

The primary goal of network segmentation is to reduce the attack surface and limit lateral movement for potential threats within the network.

Segmentation strategies begin with the identification of network assets, resources, and data, as well as an understanding of their sensitivity and importance.

Organizations should classify assets and data into different categories based on their criticality and privacy requirements.

With a clear understanding of asset classification, organizations can define access controls, security policies, and segmentation rules that align with their security objectives.

One common segmentation approach is dividing the network into zones based on function or purpose. For example, a corporate network may have separate zones for internal users, external users, guest access, and critical infrastructure.

Each zone is isolated from the others, and access is controlled through firewalls, routers, and access control lists (ACLs) to ensure that only authorized traffic is allowed between segments.

Micro-segmentation is an advanced segmentation technique that takes segmentation to a granular level by dividing a network into smaller segments, often at the individual workload or application level.

Micro-segmentation provides organizations with fine-grained control over access and security policies, reducing the lateral movement of threats within the network.

The implementation of network segmentation often begins with a thorough network architecture review and redesign, as existing network configurations may not support segmentation requirements.

Network devices such as firewalls, routers, switches, and virtualization platforms play a crucial role in enforcing segmentation rules and access controls.

Firewalls, both physical and virtual, are key components in segmentation, as they provide the necessary traffic filtering and rule enforcement between network segments.

Intrusion detection and prevention systems (IDS/IPS) can enhance network segmentation by providing real-time monitoring and threat detection at segment boundaries.

Access control mechanisms, such as role-based access control (RBAC) and identity and access management (IAM) solutions, help organizations manage user permissions and enforce access policies within segmented zones.

Network segmentation can also be complemented by network encryption techniques, such as Virtual Private Networks (VPNs) or Secure Sockets Layer (SSL) protocols, to ensure that data in transit remains secure even within segmented zones.

Segmentation strategies should consider the potential impact on network performance, as the increased use of firewalls and access controls can introduce latency and overhead.

Organizations must strike a balance between security and performance, implementing segmentation measures that protect critical assets without significantly degrading network performance.

Auditing and monitoring are essential aspects of network segmentation to ensure that policies are enforced effectively, and access controls are maintained.

Regular audits can help organizations identify misconfigurations, unauthorized access attempts, and potential security gaps within segmented zones.

Network segmentation should align with compliance requirements and industry standards, such as the Payment Card Industry Data Security Standard (PCI DSS) or the Health Insurance Portability and Accountability Act (HIPAA).

Compliance frameworks often include specific requirements for network segmentation to protect sensitive data and ensure data privacy.

When implementing segmentation, organizations should prioritize assets and data that require the highest level of protection.

Sensitive data, such as customer information, financial records, and intellectual property, should be isolated in segmented zones with the most stringent security controls.

Network segmentation should be part of a layered security strategy, complementing other security measures, such as firewall rules, intrusion detection systems, and endpoint security solutions.

Automation and orchestration tools can streamline the management and enforcement of segmentation policies, making it easier to adapt to changing network conditions and security threats.

Regular testing and validation of segmentation rules and access controls are essential to ensure that the segmentation strategy is effective and resilient to potential threats.

Segmentation strategies should consider the dynamic nature of modern networks, where devices and workloads may move across segments or between physical and virtual environments.

Organizations should implement segmentation measures that can adapt to changing network conditions and scale as needed to accommodate growth.

In summary, network segmentation strategies are vital for enhancing security by reducing the attack surface and limiting lateral movement within networks.

Organizations should classify assets and data, define access controls and security policies, and implement segmentation measures that align with their security objectives.

Segmentation can be based on function, purpose, or even granular levels like individual workloads or applications.

Firewalls, access controls, intrusion detection systems, and encryption play key roles in enforcing segmentation rules and protecting critical assets.

Network segmentation should consider performance implications, compliance requirements, and the dynamic nature of modern networks, with regular auditing and testing to ensure effectiveness.

Ultimately, a well-designed network segmentation strategy is a fundamental component of a robust cybersecurity posture, providing organizations with the necessary tools to protect their data, applications, and infrastructure from evolving threats. Micro-segmentation is a security strategy that takes network segmentation to a granular level, allowing organizations to divide their networks into small, isolated segments or zones, often at the individual workload or application level.

The concept of micro-segmentation aligns closely with the principles of Zero Trust security, which emphasizes the idea that organizations should not trust any user or device, whether they are inside or outside the network perimeter.

In a traditional network, segmentation typically occurs at a broader level, where networks are divided into segments based on function or purpose, such as separating the corporate network from the guest network or isolating sensitive data. While this provides some level of security, it may not be sufficient to protect against sophisticated cyber threats that can move laterally within a network once they breach the perimeter. Micro-segmentation, on the other hand, allows organizations to create small, isolated segments within those broader segments, adding an additional layer of security. This approach ensures that even if an attacker gains access to one segment, they will encounter further barriers when trying to move laterally within the network.

The key to micro-segmentation is the fine-grained control it offers over network traffic and access. Organizations can define specific access policies for each workload or application, specifying which resources it can communicate with and what type of traffic is allowed.

This level of control helps prevent unauthorized lateral movement within the network and limits the potential impact of a security breach.

In a Zero Trust security model, the fundamental principle is to "never trust, always verify." This means that all network traffic, regardless of its source, destination, or location within the network, should be subject to verification and authorization.

Micro-segmentation plays a crucial role in implementing the Zero Trust model by enforcing strict access controls and verification mechanisms at the micro-level.

With micro-segmentation in place, organizations can apply the principle of "least privilege access," where users or devices are only granted the minimum level of access required to perform their tasks.

This significantly reduces the attack surface and minimizes the risk of unauthorized access or lateral movement by attackers.

Micro-segmentation also provides enhanced visibility into network traffic and communication patterns. Since each workload or application operates within its isolated segment, any deviation from normal behavior can be quickly detected and investigated.

In the event of a security incident or suspicious activity, security teams can pinpoint the affected segment and take immediate action to contain and mitigate the threat.

Another advantage of micro-segmentation is its ability to support dynamic and evolving network environments. With the increasing adoption of cloud services and virtualization, network topologies can change rapidly.

Micro-segmentation allows organizations to adapt their security policies dynamically to accommodate these changes without compromising security.

In a traditional network, adjusting access controls or network policies can be a cumbersome and time-consuming process. Micro-segmentation simplifies this task by providing a flexible and scalable framework for managing security at the micro-level.

To implement micro-segmentation effectively, organizations need to have a clear understanding of their network architecture and asset inventory.

They should classify workloads and applications based on their criticality and sensitivity, identifying which assets require the highest level of protection.

Once assets are classified, organizations can define access policies and segmentation rules, specifying which workloads can communicate with each other and what types of traffic are permitted.

Micro-segmentation is typically enforced using specialized security solutions, such as micro-segmentation platforms or software-defined networking (SDN) technologies.

These solutions provide the necessary tools to create, manage, and monitor micro-segments within the network.

Organizations should regularly audit and assess their micro-segmentation policies and access controls to ensure they remain effective and aligned with security objectives.

Periodic testing and validation of segmentation rules can help identify misconfigurations or vulnerabilities.

Micro-segmentation should also align with industry-specific regulations and compliance requirements. Organizations handling sensitive data must ensure that their micro-segmentation strategy complies with relevant standards.

In summary, micro-segmentation is a powerful security strategy that aligns with the principles of Zero Trust security.

It provides organizations with fine-grained control over network traffic and access, reducing the attack surface, limiting lateral movement, and enhancing visibility into network communication patterns.

Micro-segmentation supports dynamic and evolving network environments, making it a valuable tool for modern cybersecurity.

By implementing micro-segmentation effectively, organizations can strengthen their security posture and better protect their data, applications, and infrastructure from sophisticated cyber threats.

Chapter 9: Zero Trust Security Models

Zero Trust is a cybersecurity concept and strategy that challenges the traditional security model based on the assumption that anything inside the corporate network is trusted and anything outside is not.

The central idea of Zero Trust is to "never trust, always verify," meaning that organizations should never automatically trust any user or device, whether they are inside or outside the network perimeter.

This approach recognizes that threats can come from both external and internal sources, and it places a higher emphasis on verifying identity and enforcing strict access controls.

The concept of Zero Trust was introduced by Forrester Research analyst John Kindervag in 2010, and it has since gained widespread recognition as a fundamental cybersecurity principle.

Zero Trust assumes that threats can be present both outside and inside the network, and it aims to protect against insider threats and lateral movement by attackers who have already breached the perimeter.

The implementation of Zero Trust involves a set of guiding principles and security strategies designed to reduce the attack surface, minimize the risk of unauthorized access, and enhance visibility and control over network traffic.

One of the core principles of Zero Trust is identity and access management, where user identities are verified and authenticated before granting access to resources.

This includes multi-factor authentication (MFA) and strong authentication methods to ensure that only authorized users can access systems and data.

Another fundamental principle of Zero Trust is the principle of "least privilege," which means that users and devices are granted only the minimum level of access necessary to perform their tasks.

This reduces the potential for unauthorized access and limits the impact of security breaches.

Network segmentation is a key component of Zero Trust, where the network is divided into smaller, isolated segments or zones, and access controls are enforced between these segments.

This limits the lateral movement of threats within the network and provides an additional layer of security.

Micro-segmentation, a more granular form of network segmentation, takes this concept further by dividing the network into segments at the individual workload or application level.

Micro-segmentation provides fine-grained control over access and traffic flows, reducing the attack surface even further.

Zero Trust also emphasizes continuous monitoring and real-time visibility into network traffic and user behavior.

This allows organizations to detect and respond to security incidents promptly.

Security analytics and machine learning can help identify anomalous behavior and potential threats.

Encryption and data protection are essential components of Zero Trust to ensure that sensitive data remains secure, both in transit and at rest.

Organizations should encrypt data, implement secure communication protocols, and employ encryption technologies like secure sockets layer (SSL) and transport layer security (TLS).

In a Zero Trust model, trust is never assumed, even for devices and applications within the network.

Device authentication and security posture assessment are essential to ensure that only trusted and compliant devices are allowed to connect to the network.

This includes checking the device's security configuration and patch level.

Cloud security and remote access are critical considerations in a Zero Trust environment, as more organizations rely on cloud services and remote work.

Organizations should apply Zero Trust principles to their cloud environments, enforcing strict access controls and verifying identities for cloud-based resources.

Remote access solutions should also require strong authentication and encryption to protect data during transmission.

Zero Trust extends beyond the network perimeter to include endpoints and users, making endpoint security a crucial component.

Organizations should implement security measures on endpoints, such as antivirus software, endpoint detection and response (EDR) solutions, and regular patch management.

User education and awareness are essential in a Zero Trust model, as users play a significant role in verifying their identity and following security best practices.

Training programs should cover topics like recognizing phishing attempts, using strong passwords, and reporting suspicious activities.

Zero Trust is not a one-time implementation but an ongoing process that requires continuous assessment, adjustment, and improvement.

Organizations should regularly review and update their Zero Trust strategies to adapt to changing threats and technologies.

Security assessments and penetration testing can help identify weaknesses and vulnerabilities in a Zero Trust environment.

In summary, Zero Trust is a cybersecurity concept and strategy that challenges traditional security assumptions and emphasizes the importance of verifying identity and enforcing strict access controls.

It involves principles such as identity and access management, least privilege, network segmentation, encryption, device authentication, and continuous monitoring.

Zero Trust extends to endpoints, cloud environments, and remote access solutions, making it a comprehensive approach to modern cybersecurity.

By implementing Zero Trust principles and strategies, organizations can strengthen their security posture and protect against evolving cyber threats both from outside and within the network perimeter.

Zero Trust Network Access (ZTNA) solutions are a vital component of the Zero Trust security model, offering organizations a more secure and adaptable approach to network access.

ZTNA redefines how users and devices access network resources by adopting a "never trust, always verify" philosophy, regardless of their location or the network they are connecting from.

This approach aims to minimize the attack surface, reduce the risk of unauthorized access, and enhance visibility and control over network traffic.

Traditional network access models often rely on perimeter-based security measures, where users and devices inside the corporate network are trusted, while those outside are treated as untrusted.

However, with the increasing prevalence of remote work, cloud services, and mobile devices, the traditional perimeter has become porous and less effective in defending against modern threats.

ZTNA solutions provide an alternative approach, focusing on identity and context-based access controls rather than the traditional network perimeter.

One of the key principles of ZTNA is identity-centric authentication, where users and devices must be authenticated and verified before they can access network resources.

This involves multi-factor authentication (MFA), strong authentication methods, and the use of identity providers to ensure the legitimacy of users and devices.

ZTNA also leverages the principle of "least privilege access," which means that users and devices are granted the minimum level of access required to perform their tasks, reducing the risk of unauthorized access.

Network segmentation is another fundamental component of ZTNA, where the network is divided into smaller, isolated segments, and access controls are enforced between these segments.

This limits the lateral movement of threats within the network and provides an additional layer of security.

Micro-segmentation, a more granular form of network segmentation, can be implemented within ZTNA solutions, allowing organizations to divide the network into segments at the individual workload or application level.

Micro-segmentation provides fine-grained control over access and traffic flows, reducing the attack surface even further.

Zero Trust Network Access solutions enable organizations to implement strict access controls based on user identity, device health, and contextual factors such as location, time of day, and application requirements.

These contextual factors help organizations make dynamic access decisions, ensuring that only authorized users with trusted devices can access specific resources.

ZTNA solutions also provide enhanced visibility and continuous monitoring of network traffic and user behavior, allowing organizations to detect and respond to security incidents promptly.

Security analytics and machine learning are often used to identify anomalous behavior and potential threats within the network.

Encryption and data protection are essential components of ZTNA to ensure that sensitive data remains secure, both in transit and at rest.

Organizations should employ encryption technologies like secure sockets layer (SSL) and transport layer security (TLS) to protect data during transmission.

Device authentication and security posture assessment are crucial in ZTNA to ensure that only trusted and compliant devices are allowed to connect to the network.

This includes checking the device's security configuration, patch level, and compliance with security policies.

ZTNA solutions extend beyond the traditional corporate network, making them well-suited for remote access scenarios.

Remote users can connect to the corporate network securely, with strong authentication and encryption to protect data during transmission.

Cloud security is another critical aspect of ZTNA, as organizations increasingly rely on cloud services.

ZTNA solutions can be integrated with cloud environments, enforcing strict access controls and verifying identities for cloud-based resources.

In summary, Zero Trust Network Access (ZTNA) solutions provide organizations with a more secure and adaptable approach to network access.

They adopt a "never trust, always verify" philosophy, focusing on identity-centric authentication, least privilege access, network segmentation, and dynamic access controls.

ZTNA solutions enhance visibility and monitoring, employ encryption and data protection, and support remote access and cloud security.

By implementing ZTNA, organizations can strengthen their security posture and protect against modern cyber threats while enabling flexible and secure network access for users and devices.

Chapter 10: Cyber Resilience Testing and Continuous Improvement

Cyber resilience assessment and testing frameworks are essential tools for organizations seeking to strengthen their ability to withstand and recover from cyberattacks and disruptions.

These frameworks provide structured methodologies and guidelines to assess an organization's preparedness, identify vulnerabilities, and test its response and recovery capabilities in the face of cyber incidents.

One widely recognized framework in this domain is the Cybersecurity Maturity Model Certification (CMMC), which is particularly relevant for organizations doing business with the U.S. Department of Defense.

The CMMC framework assesses an organization's cybersecurity maturity across five levels, ranging from "Basic Cyber Hygiene" to "Advanced/Progressive."

Each level includes specific practices and processes that organizations must implement and demonstrate to achieve certification.

Another notable framework is the NIST Cybersecurity Framework, developed by the National Institute of Standards and Technology (NIST).

This framework provides a comprehensive approach to managing and reducing cybersecurity risk, emphasizing five key functions: Identify, Protect, Detect, Respond, and Recover.

The NIST Cybersecurity Framework helps organizations assess their current cybersecurity posture and develop strategies to improve their resilience.

The Cybersecurity Framework for Critical Infrastructure, commonly referred to as the NIST CSF, focuses on protecting critical infrastructure sectors and assets.

Organizations within these sectors can use the framework to evaluate their cybersecurity capabilities and align them with industry best practices.

The ISO/IEC 27001 framework is another globally recognized standard for cybersecurity management.

It provides a systematic approach to managing information security, including risk assessment, risk treatment, and security controls implementation.

ISO/IEC 27001 also offers a certification process, allowing organizations to demonstrate their commitment to information security to customers and partners.

The NIST Special Publication 800-53 provides a comprehensive catalog of security and privacy controls that organizations can use to protect their systems and data.

These controls are grouped into families, covering various aspects of cybersecurity, from access control and audit and accountability to system and communications protection.

The Payment Card Industry Data Security Standard (PCI DSS) is a framework designed specifically for organizations that handle payment card data.

PCI DSS sets forth requirements and security best practices to protect cardholder information, with a focus on securing payment card transactions.

The Center for Internet Security (CIS) Controls is a prioritized set of actions that organizations can take to enhance their cybersecurity posture.

These controls are organized into three categories: basic, foundational, and organizational, providing a roadmap for improving security incrementally.

The MITRE ATT&CK framework focuses on adversary tactics, techniques, and procedures (TTPs) used in cyberattacks.

It provides organizations with insights into the methods employed by threat actors and helps them develop strategies to detect and mitigate these tactics effectively.

Penetration testing is a crucial element of cyber resilience assessment and testing.

Organizations can engage ethical hackers or security professionals to simulate cyberattacks and identify vulnerabilities in their systems, applications, and networks.

Vulnerability assessments involve scanning systems and applications to identify known vulnerabilities and weaknesses that could be exploited by attackers.

These assessments help organizations prioritize and remediate vulnerabilities to reduce their risk exposure.

Red teaming is an advanced form of assessment where a dedicated team simulates the actions of real-world attackers to test an organization's defenses and response capabilities.

Red team exercises provide a holistic view of an organization's cybersecurity readiness.

Incident response tabletop exercises involve scenarios and simulations to test an organization's incident response plan, coordination, and communication among response teams.

These exercises help identify gaps and improve incident response procedures.

Cyber resilience assessment and testing frameworks are not one-size-fits-all; organizations should choose the most appropriate framework or combination of frameworks based on their industry, regulatory requirements, and specific cybersecurity needs.

Regular assessments and testing are essential components of a proactive cybersecurity strategy, helping organizations identify weaknesses and areas for improvement before they are exploited by attackers.

While frameworks provide a structured approach, organizations should also consider the unique threats and risks they face and tailor their assessments and testing accordingly.

In summary, cyber resilience assessment and testing frameworks are valuable tools for organizations striving to enhance their cybersecurity posture and preparedness.

Frameworks like CMMC, NIST Cybersecurity Framework, ISO/IEC 27001, and others provide structured methodologies and guidelines for assessing and improving cybersecurity maturity.

These frameworks, along with penetration testing, vulnerability assessments, red teaming, and tabletop exercises, help organizations identify vulnerabilities, strengthen defenses, and improve their incident response capabilities.

By integrating these frameworks and practices into their cybersecurity strategy, organizations can better protect their systems, data, and operations from evolving cyber threats.

Establishing a culture of continuous improvement in cybersecurity is essential in today's ever-evolving threat landscape.

Cyberattacks are becoming more sophisticated and frequent, making it crucial for organizations to adapt and enhance their security measures continuously.

This culture of continuous improvement should start with leadership, as executives and managers set the tone for the entire organization.

They must prioritize cybersecurity as a core business function and communicate its importance to all employees.

Leaders should also allocate resources, both in terms of budget and personnel, to support ongoing cybersecurity initiatives and improvements.

Creating awareness and buy-in among employees is a critical step in fostering a culture of continuous improvement.

All staff members, from the IT department to non-technical personnel, should understand the role they play in cybersecurity.

Regular training and awareness programs can help employees recognize potential threats and respond effectively.

In addition to education, organizations should establish clear cybersecurity policies and procedures that are accessible to all employees.

These policies should outline expectations for responsible and secure behavior and provide guidance on reporting incidents.

To facilitate continuous improvement, organizations should conduct regular cybersecurity risk assessments.

These assessments help identify vulnerabilities, evaluate the effectiveness of existing controls, and prioritize areas for improvement.

Risk assessments should be comprehensive and consider internal and external threats, compliance requirements, and emerging technologies.

The results of risk assessments should drive action plans and initiatives to address identified weaknesses and reduce risk.

Incorporating threat intelligence into cybersecurity practices is another essential aspect of continuous improvement.

Organizations should stay informed about the latest threats and tactics used by cybercriminals.

This knowledge can inform proactive measures to strengthen defenses and protect against emerging threats.

Part of establishing a culture of continuous improvement involves embracing a proactive approach to cybersecurity.

Rather than reacting to incidents after they occur, organizations should aim to prevent them through proactive measures.

This includes implementing advanced security solutions, staying up-to-date with patch management, and regularly reviewing and improving access controls.

Continuous monitoring of network traffic and system logs is essential for detecting anomalies and potential security incidents.

By monitoring in real-time, organizations can respond swiftly to threats and mitigate their impact.

Establishing an incident response plan is a fundamental component of a cybersecurity improvement culture.

This plan should outline the steps to take when a security incident occurs, from identifying the incident to containing it and recovering affected systems.

Regularly testing and updating the incident response plan ensures that it remains effective.

Collaboration within the organization is crucial for continuous improvement.

Departments and teams should work together to share information and insights about cybersecurity threats and incidents.

Collaboration fosters a culture of collective responsibility for cybersecurity.

Auditing and assessment are valuable tools for measuring the effectiveness of cybersecurity controls and practices.

Organizations can conduct internal audits or engage external auditors to evaluate their cybersecurity programs and identify areas for improvement.

Compliance with industry-specific regulations and standards should also be a focus of continuous improvement efforts.

Ensuring that cybersecurity practices align with regulatory requirements is essential for avoiding penalties and maintaining customer trust.

External audits and assessments can provide valuable insights into compliance gaps.

In addition to external audits, organizations can participate in cybersecurity maturity assessments, which compare their cybersecurity practices to industry benchmarks and best practices.

These assessments help organizations identify areas where they may be falling behind their peers and provide a roadmap for improvement.

Regularly updating and patching software and systems is a foundational aspect of cybersecurity improvement.

Many cyberattacks exploit known vulnerabilities that could have been prevented with timely patching.

Organizations should establish patch management processes to ensure that systems are consistently updated.

Regularly testing the organization's security posture is an essential part of continuous improvement.

Penetration testing and vulnerability scanning can identify weaknesses and provide recommendations for remediation.

Red teaming exercises, where ethical hackers simulate real-world attacks, can challenge existing defenses and identify areas for improvement.

Finally, fostering a culture of continuous improvement requires organizations to stay adaptable and agile.

The cybersecurity landscape is constantly evolving, and what works today may not be effective tomorrow.

Organizations must be open to change and willing to adjust their cybersecurity strategies and practices as new threats and technologies emerge.

In summary, establishing a culture of continuous improvement in cybersecurity is essential for organizations to effectively protect their systems, data, and operations in an evolving threat landscape.

Leadership, employee awareness, proactive measures, risk assessments, threat intelligence, incident response, collaboration, auditing, compliance, external assessments, patch management, and regular testing are all crucial components of this culture.

By embracing continuous improvement and remaining adaptable, organizations can better safeguard their digital assets and respond effectively to emerging cyber threats.

BOOK 3
FROM NOVICE TO NINJA
THE COMPREHENSIVE GUIDE TO DEFENSE IN DEPTH IN NETWORK SECURITY

ROB BOTWRIGHT

Chapter 1: Foundations of Network Security

The historical evolution of network security reflects the dynamic and ever-changing nature of information technology.

From the early days of computer networks to the complex and interconnected digital world we now inhabit, network security has continually adapted to address evolving threats and challenges.

In the early 1970s, when computer networks were in their infancy, the primary concern was ensuring the confidentiality and integrity of data.

At that time, security measures consisted of basic access controls and encryption techniques.

With the advent of the internet in the late 20th century, the landscape of network security changed dramatically.

The internet brought new opportunities for communication and commerce, but it also introduced a host of new vulnerabilities and threats.

One of the earliest security protocols, the Secure Sockets Layer (SSL), was developed in the mid-1990s to secure online transactions and protect data in transit.

SSL laid the foundation for the modern Transport Layer Security (TLS) protocol, which is still used today to secure internet communications.

The late 1990s and early 2000s saw the rise of firewalls as a critical component of network security.

Firewalls were designed to protect internal networks from unauthorized access and malicious traffic from the internet.

These early firewalls used static rules to filter traffic, but as the internet evolved, so did the sophistication of attacks.

In response, next-generation firewalls (NGFWs) were developed, incorporating advanced features like intrusion detection and prevention, deep packet inspection, and application-layer filtering.

Around the same time, virtual private networks (VPNs) became widely used to secure remote access to corporate networks.

VPNs use encryption to create a secure tunnel for data transmission over untrusted networks, such as the internet.

As e-commerce and online banking grew, so did the need for strong authentication methods.

Usernames and passwords were no longer sufficient, leading to the adoption of multi-factor authentication (MFA) and biometric authentication.

The early 2000s also witnessed the emergence of antivirus software as a fundamental security tool.

Antivirus programs were designed to detect and remove known malware and viruses from computer systems.

However, attackers continued to evolve their tactics, and new forms of malware posed significant challenges.

The rise of mobile devices in the 2000s introduced a new dimension to network security.

Smartphones and tablets became popular targets for cybercriminals, leading to the development of mobile security solutions and the concept of mobile device management (MDM).

In the mid-2000s, the concept of network segmentation gained prominence as a strategy to limit the impact of security breaches.

Segmentation divides a network into smaller, isolated segments, reducing lateral movement by attackers.

In parallel, the field of intrusion detection and prevention systems (IDPS) saw significant advances.

IDPS solutions evolved to detect and respond to sophisticated threats in real-time.

In the early 2010s, cloud computing gained momentum, revolutionizing how organizations managed and accessed their data and applications.

While cloud services offered many advantages, they also raised concerns about data security and privacy.

Security in the cloud became a top priority, leading to the development of cloud security solutions and best practices.

The growing threat landscape, including advanced persistent threats (APTs) and nation-state-sponsored cyberattacks, prompted organizations to adopt a more proactive approach to cybersecurity.

Threat intelligence services emerged to provide organizations with timely information about emerging threats and vulnerabilities.

Security information and event management (SIEM) systems became essential for monitoring and analyzing network activity, helping organizations detect and respond to security incidents.

As the internet of things (IoT) gained momentum, the need for securing connected devices became apparent.

IoT security focuses on safeguarding the vast array of interconnected devices and sensors, which can be vulnerable to attacks.

The introduction of the General Data Protection Regulation (GDPR) in 2018 marked a significant shift in data protection and privacy regulations.

GDPR mandated stringent data protection practices and put organizations under strict compliance requirements.

The proliferation of cloud-native technologies and containerization introduced new challenges in securing dynamic and elastic environments.

Security solutions like container security platforms and cloud security posture management (CSPM) tools emerged to address these challenges.

In recent years, the concept of zero trust security gained traction as organizations recognized the need to verify trustworthiness continuously, both inside and outside their networks.

Zero trust architectures focus on identity and context-based access controls.

Today, the evolving landscape of network security encompasses a wide array of technologies and practices, from artificial intelligence and machine learning to threat hunting and incident response orchestration.

Cybersecurity has become a critical aspect of business operations, and organizations must adapt and invest in security measures that keep pace with the ever-evolving threat landscape.

The historical evolution of network security reflects the ongoing battle between security practitioners and cybercriminals, with each advancement in security met by increasingly sophisticated attacks.

As organizations move forward, they must continue to innovate and adopt a proactive, holistic approach to cybersecurity to protect their digital assets and maintain trust in the digital age.

Network security is a complex and critical field that encompasses a set of key principles to protect digital assets, data, and communications.

At its core, network security aims to safeguard the confidentiality, integrity, and availability of information.

Confidentiality ensures that only authorized individuals or systems can access sensitive data.

Integrity guarantees that data remains unaltered during transmission or storage, preventing unauthorized modifications.

Availability ensures that information and services are accessible when needed, without disruption.

To achieve these goals, network security operates on several fundamental principles.

One of the foundational principles is the principle of defense in depth.

Defense in depth is a layered approach to security that deploys multiple security measures across the network.

This principle acknowledges that no single security solution can provide complete protection.

Instead, it advocates a combination of measures, such as firewalls, intrusion detection systems, encryption, and access controls, to create multiple barriers that an attacker must overcome.

Another essential principle is the principle of least privilege.

This principle emphasizes restricting access rights for users, systems, and processes to the minimum necessary for their tasks.

By limiting privileges, organizations reduce the potential for unauthorized access and minimize the impact of security breaches.

Authentication and authorization are crucial components of implementing the principle of least privilege.

Authentication verifies the identity of users, devices, or systems, ensuring they are who they claim to be.

Authorization determines the access rights and permissions granted to authenticated entities.

Encryption is a fundamental principle of network security that ensures data confidentiality.

Encryption transforms data into an unreadable format that can only be deciphered by authorized parties with the appropriate decryption keys.

It protects sensitive information from eavesdropping and interception during transmission or storage.

Key management is an integral part of encryption, ensuring that encryption keys are securely generated, stored, and distributed.

Network segmentation is another key principle that divides a network into smaller, isolated segments or subnetworks.

Each segment has its security controls, reducing the attack surface and containing potential security incidents.

Segmentation limits lateral movement by attackers, preventing them from easily traversing the network.

Monitoring and logging are essential principles that involve continuous tracking of network activity.

Monitoring identifies suspicious or malicious behavior, while logging records network events for later analysis.

Security information and event management (SIEM) systems collect and analyze logs, providing insights into potential security threats and incidents.

Vulnerability management is a proactive principle focused on identifying and mitigating weaknesses in the network.

Regular vulnerability assessments and scans help organizations discover vulnerabilities and apply patches or remediation measures promptly.

Patch management is closely related to vulnerability management, as it ensures that security patches and updates are applied to systems and software promptly.

Failure to patch known vulnerabilities can leave systems exposed to exploitation.

Regular updates and patching are essential for maintaining network security.

Access control is a fundamental principle that governs who can access specific resources and under what conditions.

Access control includes user authentication, authorization, and the enforcement of security policies.

Firewalls are a critical element of network security that enforce access control policies by examining and filtering network traffic.

Firewalls can be hardware or software-based and are positioned at network boundaries to inspect and permit or deny traffic based on defined rules.

Intrusion detection and prevention systems (IDPS) are designed to identify and respond to suspicious or malicious activities within a network.

IDPS solutions use a combination of signature-based detection, anomaly detection, and behavior analysis to detect and mitigate threats.

Two-factor authentication (2FA) or multi-factor authentication (MFA) is a security principle that adds an extra layer of verification beyond traditional username and password authentication.

2FA requires users to provide two or more authentication factors, such as something they know (password) and something they have (smart card or mobile device).

Security awareness and training are essential principles that educate users about security best practices and potential threats.

Aware and informed users are less likely to fall victim to social engineering attacks, such as phishing or pretexting.

Incident response is a principle that outlines the procedures and actions to take when a security incident occurs.

A well-defined incident response plan helps organizations minimize the impact of security breaches, recover quickly, and learn from the experience.

Regular testing and drills of the incident response plan ensure that the organization can effectively respond to security incidents.

Business continuity and disaster recovery are principles that focus on maintaining essential operations and data availability in the face of disruptions or disasters.

These principles involve creating and testing plans to recover from various scenarios, including natural disasters, cyberattacks, and equipment failures.

Auditing and compliance are principles that ensure organizations adhere to industry regulations, standards, and internal policies.

Regular audits and compliance assessments help organizations identify areas where they may be falling short and make necessary improvements.

Lastly, risk management is a fundamental principle that involves identifying, assessing, and mitigating risks to the network.

This principle guides organizations in making informed decisions about security investments and resource allocation.

In summary, network security is built on a set of key principles that collectively aim to protect data, systems, and communications.

These principles, such as defense in depth, least privilege, encryption, monitoring, vulnerability management, and access control, provide a comprehensive framework for securing networks in an ever-evolving threat landscape.

By adhering to these principles and continuously adapting to emerging threats, organizations can enhance their network security posture and reduce the risk of cyberattacks and data breaches.

Chapter 2: Understanding the Threat Landscape

In the ever-evolving landscape of cybersecurity, various types of threat actors pose significant challenges and threats to organizations and individuals alike.

Understanding the motivations, tactics, and characteristics of these threat actors is essential for effective cybersecurity defense.

One of the most prominent categories of threat actors is cybercriminals, individuals or groups primarily motivated by financial gain.

Cybercriminals engage in a wide range of illegal activities, including data theft, identity theft, ransomware attacks, and credit card fraud.

They often exploit vulnerabilities in systems and networks to steal valuable data or extort money from victims.

Hacktivists represent another category of threat actors who use cyberattacks to promote political or social causes.

Their motivations are typically ideological, and they aim to raise awareness or cause disruption through their actions.

Hacktivists may deface websites, launch distributed denial-of-service (DDoS) attacks, or leak sensitive information to achieve their objectives.

State-sponsored or nation-state actors are a highly sophisticated and well-resourced category of threat actors.

These actors operate on behalf of governments or intelligence agencies and engage in cyber espionage, cyber warfare, and influence campaigns.

Their primary goal is to advance their nation's interests by stealing sensitive information, disrupting critical infrastructure, or spreading disinformation.

Insiders, including employees and trusted individuals within organizations, can also pose a significant cybersecurity threat.

Insider threats can be malicious or unintentional, and they involve the misuse of privileges or access to carry out attacks or expose sensitive information.

Malware authors and developers are individuals or groups responsible for creating and distributing malicious software, known as malware.

Malware includes viruses, worms, Trojans, ransomware, and spyware, among others.

These threat actors profit from infecting devices and systems, often by stealing data, extorting victims, or using compromised devices for further attacks.

Script kiddies are less sophisticated threat actors who lack the technical skills and knowledge of more advanced hackers.

They typically use pre-written scripts or tools to carry out attacks without a deep understanding of the underlying technologies.

Script kiddies may engage in defacement, DDoS attacks, or basic forms of cybercrime for personal satisfaction or recognition.

Organized crime groups are involved in various cybercrimes, such as online fraud, identity theft, and the sale of stolen data on the dark web.

These groups operate like traditional criminal organizations, with hierarchies and specialized roles.

They often collaborate with other threat actors or purchase hacking services to achieve their criminal objectives.

Extremist groups and terrorists have turned to the internet as a platform for communication, recruitment, and propaganda.

They may use social media, encrypted messaging apps, or hacking to advance their agendas, including inciting violence or spreading extremist ideologies.

A relatively recent category of threat actors is the insider-as-a-service, where malicious actors offer their insider knowledge and access to assist cybercriminals.

These individuals may have privileged access within organizations or specialized expertise that can be leveraged by cybercriminals for financial gain or corporate espionage.

Finally, there are also independent security researchers and ethical hackers who actively seek vulnerabilities to improve cybersecurity.

These individuals, often referred to as white hat hackers or security experts, help organizations identify and patch vulnerabilities before malicious threat actors can exploit them.

While they have good intentions, ethical hackers must operate within legal and ethical boundaries.

In summary, the diverse landscape of cyber threat actors encompasses a range of motivations, tactics, and characteristics.

Cybercriminals seek financial gain, hacktivists pursue ideological causes, state-sponsored actors engage in espionage and cyber warfare, and insiders pose both intentional and unintentional risks.

Malware authors, script kiddies, organized crime groups, extremist organizations, and insider-as-a-service actors each contribute to the complexity of the threat landscape.

Meanwhile, ethical hackers and security researchers play a crucial role in improving cybersecurity.

Understanding the various types of threat actors and their motivations is essential for organizations and individuals to implement effective cybersecurity strategies and defenses. As the field of cybersecurity continues to evolve, it is essential to stay vigilant and adapt to emerging threat trends and patterns. Cyber threats are dynamic and constantly changing, driven by advances in technology, shifts in the digital landscape, and evolving tactics of malicious actors.

One notable emerging threat trend is the rise of ransomware attacks. Ransomware is a type of malware that encrypts a victim's data and demands a ransom payment in exchange for the decryption key. These attacks have grown in scale and sophistication, targeting not only individuals but also organizations, healthcare providers, and critical infrastructure. Ransomware attackers often demand cryptocurrency payments to make tracing and prosecution more challenging. The use of cryptocurrency in cybercrime is another emerging trend that poses challenges for law enforcement and cybersecurity professionals.

Cryptocurrencies provide a level of anonymity that makes it difficult to trace financial transactions involved in cyberattacks, money laundering, and ransom payments.

This anonymity has facilitated the growth of ransomware attacks and cybercriminal enterprises.

Supply chain attacks have also gained prominence as a concerning trend in cybersecurity.

Malicious actors are increasingly targeting software vendors and suppliers to compromise widely used applications.

By infiltrating the supply chain, attackers can distribute malware or backdoors to unsuspecting customers, creating a significant security risk.

Nation-state-sponsored cyberattacks remain a persistent threat trend, with governments using cyber capabilities for espionage, influence campaigns, and potential disruption of critical infrastructure.

These attacks are often highly sophisticated and well-coordinated, making them challenging to defend against.

Social engineering attacks, such as phishing and spear-phishing, continue to be effective methods for cybercriminals to gain access to systems and sensitive information.

These attacks exploit human psychology and trust, making individuals the weakest link in many security strategies.

Phishing campaigns have become more targeted and convincing, often impersonating trusted organizations and using advanced social engineering techniques.

One of the emerging threat trends in recent years is the increasing number of IoT (Internet of Things) devices that are susceptible to attacks.

IoT devices, ranging from smart home appliances to industrial sensors, often lack robust security measures and are vulnerable to exploitation.

Compromised IoT devices can be harnessed to create botnets for large-scale DDoS (Distributed Denial of Service) attacks or used as entry points into networks.

Deepfake technology represents another concerning trend in the realm of cyber threats.

Deepfakes involve the use of artificial intelligence to manipulate audio and video content to create convincing but entirely fabricated media.

This technology can be used for disinformation campaigns, fake news, and impersonation attacks.

The increasing adoption of cloud services and the migration of data and applications to the cloud have also created new threat vectors.

Misconfigured cloud environments and inadequate security measures can lead to data breaches and unauthorized access.

Cloud service providers offer security tools, but it is the responsibility of organizations to configure and manage their cloud resources securely.

Another emerging threat pattern is the exploitation of vulnerabilities in critical infrastructure systems, such as power grids, water treatment facilities, and transportation networks.

Attacks on critical infrastructure can have severe consequences, impacting public safety and national security.

To combat these emerging threats, cybersecurity professionals and organizations must adopt a proactive and adaptive approach.

This approach includes continuous monitoring of network traffic, threat intelligence sharing, regular vulnerability assessments, and employee training and awareness programs.

Organizations should also implement robust incident response plans to mitigate the impact of cyberattacks and ensure business continuity.

Collaboration and information sharing within the cybersecurity community and across industries are essential to stay ahead of evolving threats.

Government agencies, law enforcement, and international organizations play a vital role in addressing nation-state-sponsored cyber threats and promoting global cybersecurity cooperation.

As technology continues to advance, new threat trends and patterns will continue to emerge.

Cybersecurity professionals must remain vigilant, adaptable, and committed to protecting digital assets and maintaining the integrity of the digital landscape.

Chapter 3: Network Design for Defense in Depth

Network security relies heavily on secure topologies and architectures to protect critical data and systems from a wide range of threats.

The design of a network's topology and architecture is a fundamental aspect of its security posture, encompassing various elements and principles.

One crucial concept in secure network design is the concept of network segmentation.

Network segmentation involves dividing a network into smaller, isolated segments or subnetworks to limit the scope of potential security breaches.

Each segment typically has its security controls and access policies, which help prevent unauthorized lateral movement within the network.

One common approach to network segmentation is using virtual LANs (VLANs) or physical separation with routers and firewalls.

Segmentation enhances security by containing threats and isolating compromised systems, making it more challenging for attackers to move freely within the network.

Another key principle in secure network design is the implementation of a perimeter security layer.

The perimeter security layer serves as the first line of defense against external threats.

Firewalls, intrusion detection systems (IDS), intrusion prevention systems (IPS), and web application firewalls (WAF) are often deployed at the network perimeter to filter incoming and outgoing traffic, detect suspicious activities, and block malicious content.

Intrusion detection and prevention systems monitor network traffic for signs of malicious activity, while web application firewalls protect web applications from common web-based attacks.

The use of demilitarized zones (DMZs) is a common architectural practice in secure network design.

DMZs are isolated network segments located between the internal network and the external network, typically the internet.

DMZs host services that need to be publicly accessible, such as web servers, while providing an additional layer of security.

Secure network architectures often incorporate the principle of redundancy and failover to ensure high availability and resilience.

Redundant components, such as multiple routers, switches, and internet connections, can take over in case of a component failure, minimizing downtime and disruption.

Failover mechanisms are designed to automatically switch traffic to redundant components when an issue is detected.

Virtualization technologies, such as virtual private clouds (VPCs) and virtual local area networks (VLANs), enable organizations to create isolated environments within their networks.

These virtualized segments provide enhanced security by isolating different types of traffic, applications, or user groups.

Secure network architectures also emphasize the importance of access control and authentication.

Access control policies dictate who can access specific network resources and what actions they are allowed to perform.

Strong authentication methods, including multi-factor authentication (MFA), ensure that only authorized users can access sensitive systems and data.

Another critical component of secure network design is the consideration of internal threats.

Insiders with privileged access can pose a significant risk to network security.

To mitigate this risk, organizations implement strict access controls, monitor user activities, and conduct periodic audits.

Security information and event management (SIEM) systems play a crucial role in monitoring and alerting organizations to suspicious or anomalous network activities.

Regularly reviewing and analyzing SIEM logs and alerts helps detect and respond to security incidents promptly.

Secure network design also includes the principle of least privilege.

This principle limits user and system permissions to the minimum necessary to perform their tasks, reducing the potential for misuse or exploitation.

By implementing the principle of least privilege, organizations minimize the attack surface and limit the damage that can be caused by compromised accounts.

Encryption is another fundamental aspect of secure network architectures.

Encrypting data in transit and at rest ensures the confidentiality and integrity of sensitive information.

Secure sockets layer (SSL) and transport layer security (TLS) protocols are commonly used to encrypt data transmitted over the internet, while disk encryption protects data stored on devices and servers.

Additionally, secure network designs incorporate security policies and procedures that guide the deployment, management, and maintenance of security controls and measures.

These policies define acceptable use, incident response procedures, data retention policies, and other essential aspects of network security.

Finally, secure network architectures are adaptable and responsive to emerging threats.

Threat landscapes evolve, and new vulnerabilities are discovered regularly.

To remain effective, secure network designs should be flexible enough to accommodate security updates, patches, and changes in response to evolving threats.

Regular security assessments, penetration testing, and vulnerability scanning help identify and address weaknesses in network architecture.

In summary, secure network topologies and architectures are critical components of effective cybersecurity.

These designs incorporate principles such as network segmentation, perimeter security, redundancy, access control, encryption, and adaptability to create a robust defense against a wide range of threats.

By implementing these principles and continually assessing and improving network security, organizations can protect their valuable data and systems in an ever-evolving threat landscape.

Implementing network segmentation is a critical strategy for achieving defense in depth in cybersecurity.

Network segmentation involves dividing a network into smaller, isolated segments or subnetworks to enhance security.

Each segment operates independently with its own set of security controls, reducing the potential impact of security breaches.

Segmentation is a proactive approach that limits lateral movement for attackers within a network.

The primary goal of network segmentation is to minimize the attack surface and compartmentalize sensitive resources.

One common way to implement network segmentation is through the use of VLANs, or Virtual Local Area Networks.

VLANs allow organizations to create logical subnetworks within a physical network infrastructure.

By isolating groups of devices into separate VLANs, organizations can restrict access between segments.

For example, sensitive financial data can be placed in one VLAN, while guest Wi-Fi access is in another, preventing unauthorized access.

Firewalls are crucial components in implementing network segmentation.

They act as gatekeepers between segments, controlling the flow of traffic and enforcing security policies.

Firewalls can be deployed as physical appliances or as software-based solutions.

They examine incoming and outgoing traffic, blocking unauthorized access and malicious activities.

Intrusion detection and prevention systems (IDS/IPS) complement firewalls by actively monitoring network traffic for signs of suspicious behavior.

IDS systems analyze traffic patterns and generate alerts when anomalies are detected, while IPS systems can take automated actions to block or mitigate threats.

When designing network segmentation, it's essential to consider the specific requirements and security policies of the organization.

For example, organizations may segment their network based on departments, compliance regulations, or the sensitivity of data.

Critical servers or databases often reside in highly secure segments, while less sensitive resources are placed in less restrictive ones.

The design should balance security with operational efficiency to ensure that legitimate communication can still occur as needed.

Access control lists (ACLs) are another tool used to enforce segmentation policies.

ACLs specify which devices or users are allowed or denied access to specific segments or resources.

They are applied at the router or firewall level and serve as a granular control mechanism.

Implementing network segmentation can significantly reduce the attack surface and limit lateral movement for attackers.

Even if one segment is compromised, it becomes challenging for attackers to access other parts of the network.

Organizations must regularly review and update their segmentation policies and access controls to adapt to changing security threats.

Monitoring and visibility are crucial aspects of effective network segmentation.

Organizations need tools and solutions that provide visibility into network traffic, allowing them to detect and respond to security incidents promptly.

Security information and event management (SIEM) systems play a vital role in monitoring and correlating data from different segments to identify potential threats.

Regularly analyzing SIEM logs helps organizations gain insights into network behavior and identify suspicious activities.

Threat intelligence feeds can also enhance security by providing information about emerging threats and vulnerabilities relevant to the segmented network.

It's important to note that while network segmentation is an effective security strategy, it is not a standalone solution.

It should be part of a broader defense-in-depth approach that includes other security measures like encryption, strong authentication, and regular security assessments.

Furthermore, organizations must invest in employee training and awareness to prevent social engineering attacks that can bypass technical defenses.

Collaboration among IT and security teams is essential when implementing and managing network segmentation.

IT teams are responsible for configuring and maintaining the network infrastructure, while security teams define the segmentation policies and monitor for security incidents.

Communication and coordination between these teams are vital to ensuring that segmentation is implemented correctly and remains effective.

In summary, implementing network segmentation is a fundamental strategy for achieving defense in depth in cybersecurity.

It involves dividing a network into isolated segments, using tools like VLANs, firewalls, and access controls.

Segmentation helps minimize the attack surface, limit lateral movement for attackers, and protect sensitive resources.

However, it should be part of a broader security strategy that includes monitoring, threat intelligence, and user awareness to create a robust defense against evolving threats.

Chapter 4: Advanced Firewall Configuration

Advanced firewall rules and policies are essential components of a comprehensive network security strategy.

Firewalls serve as a critical barrier between an organization's internal network and the external world, effectively acting as gatekeepers for network traffic.

While basic firewall rules are designed to permit or deny traffic based on source and destination IP addresses and ports, advanced firewall rules and policies enable organizations to implement more granular and sophisticated security controls.

Advanced firewall rules can be configured to inspect traffic at deeper levels, allowing organizations to make decisions based on various factors, including application type, content, and user identity.

These rules are instrumental in ensuring that only authorized traffic is allowed while blocking or inspecting potentially malicious or unwanted traffic.

One of the key benefits of advanced firewall rules is their ability to understand and manage specific applications or services running over standard ports.

For example, a traditional firewall rule might allow traffic on port 80, commonly used for HTTP traffic, to pass through.

However, advanced firewall rules can inspect the traffic on port 80 and differentiate between regular web browsing and potentially harmful web applications or threats.

This granular control allows organizations to permit legitimate web traffic while blocking access to malicious websites or applications that could compromise security.

Furthermore, advanced firewall rules can provide deep packet inspection capabilities, allowing firewalls to analyze the content of data packets traversing the network.

This inspection can identify and block traffic containing malware, viruses, or other malicious payloads, even if they are hidden within seemingly innocuous protocols.

For example, an advanced firewall might detect and block a file transfer over the HTTP protocol if it identifies the transfer of a known malware file.

Intrusion detection and prevention capabilities are often integrated into advanced firewall policies.

Intrusion detection systems (IDS) can monitor network traffic for patterns or behaviors consistent with known attack signatures.

If a potential threat is detected, the firewall can generate alerts or take actions such as blocking the malicious traffic.

Intrusion prevention systems (IPS) go a step further by actively blocking or mitigating threats as they are detected, preventing potential security breaches.

Advanced firewall policies also enable organizations to enforce security policies based on user identity.

This is particularly important in environments where user authentication and access control are critical.

Firewalls can integrate with authentication services like LDAP, Active Directory, or Single Sign-On (SSO) to enforce policies based on specific user accounts or groups.

For example, a firewall can allow access to certain applications or services for employees while restricting access for contractors or guests.

In addition to user-based policies, advanced firewall rules can enforce policies based on device characteristics, such as device type, operating system, or compliance status.

This is especially relevant in modern Bring Your Own Device (BYOD) environments, where a wide range of devices with varying security postures may access the network.

By inspecting and classifying devices, firewalls can apply different policies to ensure that security requirements are met.

Furthermore, advanced firewall rules can facilitate secure remote access through Virtual Private Networks (VPNs) or secure tunneling protocols.

Organizations can define policies to control and secure remote connections, ensuring that remote users or branch offices connect securely and only access the resources they are authorized to use.

Additionally, firewalls can support advanced threat intelligence feeds, which provide real-time information about emerging threats and malicious IP addresses.

These feeds enable firewalls to block traffic from known malicious sources or take actions to protect the network from threats in real-time.

Firewall rules can also include time-based or scheduled policies, allowing organizations to implement different rules during specific hours or days.

For example, an organization might restrict access to certain resources during non-working hours or enforce stricter policies during weekends.

Logging and reporting capabilities are integral to advanced firewall policies.

Firewalls generate logs that capture detailed information about network traffic, policy violations, and security incidents.

These logs are essential for monitoring and auditing network activity, as well as for incident response and forensic analysis in the event of a security breach.

Advanced firewall rules can specify how logs are generated, stored, and analyzed, ensuring that security teams have the information they need to identify and mitigate threats.

In summary, advanced firewall rules and policies are crucial for implementing robust network security measures.

These rules enable organizations to define granular security controls based on application type, content, user identity, device characteristics, and more.

By leveraging advanced firewall capabilities, organizations can strengthen their defense against a wide range of cyber threats and security risks while maintaining the flexibility needed for modern network environments.

Application Layer Firewall Inspection, often referred to as Deep Packet Inspection (DPI), is a critical security mechanism that operates at the highest layer of the OSI model.

It is designed to inspect and analyze data packets at a level that traditional firewalls cannot reach.

Unlike basic packet-filtering firewalls, which operate primarily at the network and transport layers, application layer firewalls examine the content and context of packets to make informed decisions about whether to allow or block traffic.

This deep level of inspection provides enhanced security by understanding the specific applications or services that traffic represents.

Application layer firewalls are aware of the protocols and applications that traverse the network, making them capable of enforcing security policies based on this awareness.

They can identify and control applications by looking at various attributes within the packets, such as the destination port, the application protocol, and even the content of the data payload.

For example, if an organization wants to allow HTTP traffic but block access to specific websites or web applications, an application layer firewall can inspect the HTTP requests and responses to identify the URLs being accessed and take action accordingly.

This level of granularity allows organizations to enforce strict security policies while still allowing legitimate applications to function.

One key benefit of application layer firewall inspection is its ability to detect and block evasive or non-standard traffic.

Attackers often try to exploit vulnerabilities or deliver malware through non-standard or obfuscated protocols.

Traditional firewalls may not recognize these threats, as they rely on well-known port numbers and protocol signatures.

In contrast, application layer firewalls can inspect the actual content of the data packets and identify suspicious patterns or behaviors that may indicate an attack.

For example, an application layer firewall can detect SQL injection attempts or buffer overflow attacks by analyzing the content of database queries or input data.

Moreover, application layer firewall inspection plays a crucial role in preventing data leakage and ensuring compliance with data protection regulations.

Organizations can define policies to inspect and control the transfer of sensitive or confidential information over the network.

This includes identifying and blocking attempts to send credit card numbers, social security numbers, or other regulated data through email, file transfers, or web applications.

By inspecting the content of outbound traffic, application layer firewalls can enforce data loss prevention (DLP) policies and protect against data breaches.

Another important aspect of application layer firewall inspection is the ability to detect and block malicious content or malware.

Firewalls can integrate with antivirus and anti-malware engines to scan incoming and outgoing files and attachments for known malware signatures.

Additionally, they can analyze the behavior of files and scripts in real-time to identify suspicious activities that may indicate the presence of new or zero-day threats.

For example, if a file downloaded from the internet attempts to execute malicious code on the user's system, the firewall can intervene and block the file from running.

Application layer firewalls also provide advanced threat protection by inspecting encrypted traffic.

While encryption is essential for securing data in transit, it can also be used by attackers to hide malicious activities.

Firewalls can decrypt and inspect encrypted traffic, ensuring that it does not contain threats or violations of security policies.

This is particularly important in an era where the majority of internet traffic is encrypted using protocols like SSL/TLS.

Furthermore, application layer firewall inspection enables organizations to enforce application-level access controls and authentication.

Administrators can define policies that require users or devices to authenticate before accessing specific applications or services.

This adds an extra layer of security by ensuring that only authorized individuals can use critical business applications.

Additionally, it can help prevent unauthorized access to sensitive information and resources.

In summary, application layer firewall inspection is a crucial component of modern network security.

It provides granular control over network traffic by inspecting and understanding the content, context, and behavior of data packets.

This deep inspection capability allows organizations to enforce security policies based on applications, protocols, and content, enhancing protection against a wide range of threats, including malware, data breaches, and application vulnerabilities.

By combining application layer firewall inspection with other security measures, organizations can build a robust defense against evolving cyber threats while maintaining the flexibility needed to support their business operations.

Chapter 5: Intrusion Detection and Prevention Systems Mastery

In-depth intrusion detection techniques are a vital component of a modern cybersecurity strategy.

They play a crucial role in identifying and responding to unauthorized access attempts, malicious activities, and security breaches within an organization's network.

Intrusion detection is the process of monitoring network and system activities to detect suspicious or unauthorized behavior.

It involves collecting and analyzing data from various sources to identify potential security incidents.

One common approach to intrusion detection is the use of signature-based detection methods.

These methods involve comparing network traffic or system events to a database of known attack signatures or patterns.

When a match is found, the intrusion detection system (IDS) generates an alert, indicating a potential security threat.

Signature-based detection is effective at identifying well-known and previously documented attacks.

However, it may struggle to detect new or evolving threats that do not match existing signatures.

To address this limitation, anomaly-based intrusion detection techniques are employed.

Anomaly-based detection involves establishing a baseline of normal network and system behavior.

The IDS continuously monitors activities and compares them to this baseline.

If any deviations from the norm are detected, the system generates an alert.

Anomaly-based detection is valuable for identifying previously unseen or zero-day attacks.

However, it can also generate false positives if the baseline is not accurately calibrated or if legitimate changes in network behavior occur.

To enhance the accuracy of intrusion detection, hybrid approaches combine both signature-based and anomaly-based techniques.

These approaches provide a more comprehensive view of network activity and can better differentiate between known threats and unusual but legitimate behavior.

Network-based intrusion detection systems (NIDS) focus on monitoring network traffic to identify potential threats.

They examine packets as they traverse the network and can identify suspicious patterns or activities.

Host-based intrusion detection systems (HIDS), on the other hand, focus on the activities occurring on individual hosts or endpoints.

They analyze system logs, application logs, and system events to detect signs of compromise or unauthorized access.

HIDS is particularly useful for identifying insider threats and attacks that target specific systems or applications.

Intrusion detection systems can also be categorized based on their deployment location.

For example, perimeter-based IDS are placed at the network perimeter, often in front of firewalls, to monitor traffic entering and leaving the network.

These systems are well-suited for identifying external threats and attacks targeting the network's edge.

Internal IDS are positioned within the internal network, allowing them to monitor activities within the organization's trusted boundary.

They are essential for identifying insider threats and lateral movement by attackers who have already gained access to the network.

Intrusion detection techniques can also be classified based on the scope of their analysis.

Some IDS focus on specific areas, such as network traffic analysis or host-based events, while others provide broader coverage by integrating multiple data sources.

Intrusion detection systems can operate in real-time, generating alerts and taking automated actions as soon as a threat is detected.

Alternatively, they can operate in a near-real-time mode, collecting and analyzing data at regular intervals, which is then reviewed by security analysts.

Intrusion detection techniques also include behavior-based detection, which examines the behavior of users or entities within the network.

This approach can identify anomalies in user behavior, such as sudden changes in access patterns or unusual data transfer activities.

Behavior-based detection is valuable for detecting insider threats and account compromise.

To enhance the effectiveness of intrusion detection, organizations often implement correlation and aggregation techniques.

These methods involve combining data from multiple sources and analyzing it to identify complex attack patterns that may span across different parts of the network.

Intrusion detection systems can also leverage threat intelligence feeds to enhance their ability to detect and respond to emerging threats.

These feeds provide real-time information about known threats, vulnerabilities, and malicious IP addresses, allowing IDS to take proactive measures.

Furthermore, machine learning and artificial intelligence are increasingly used to improve intrusion detection.

These technologies can analyze large volumes of data, detect subtle patterns, and adapt to evolving threats.

Machine learning models can learn from historical data and continuously improve their detection capabilities.

Intrusion detection is a critical component of a broader cybersecurity strategy that includes prevention, response, and recovery.

It plays a crucial role in identifying security incidents promptly, allowing organizations to take appropriate actions to mitigate risks and minimize the impact of breaches.

In summary, in-depth intrusion detection techniques encompass various methods and approaches to monitor network and system activities, detect potential threats, and generate alerts or responses.

These techniques include signature-based, anomaly-based, and hybrid methods, as well as network-based and host-based approaches.

Intrusion detection systems can operate in real-time or near-real-time, and they may focus on specific areas or provide broader coverage.

Behavior-based detection, threat intelligence, and machine learning enhance the effectiveness of intrusion detection.

When integrated into a comprehensive cybersecurity strategy, intrusion detection plays a vital role in safeguarding organizations against a wide range of security threats.

Advanced intrusion prevention strategies are a crucial element of a modern cybersecurity posture, designed to proactively defend against a wide range of threats and security breaches.

Intrusion prevention aims to stop malicious activities before they can compromise the security of an organization's network and systems.

While intrusion detection techniques focus on identifying and alerting on potential threats, intrusion prevention systems (IPS) take a more active approach by actively blocking or mitigating those threats in real-time.

One of the key principles of advanced intrusion prevention strategies is the use of signature-based detection methods.

These methods involve comparing network traffic or system events to a database of known attack signatures or patterns.

When a match is found, the IPS can take immediate action, such as blocking the malicious traffic or triggering an alert for further investigation.

Signature-based intrusion prevention is highly effective at identifying and blocking known threats, including well-documented malware, exploits, and attack techniques.

However, it may struggle to detect new or previously unseen threats that do not match existing signatures.

To address this limitation, anomaly-based intrusion prevention techniques are often employed.

Anomaly-based IPS establishes a baseline of normal network and system behavior and continuously monitors activities against this baseline.

If any deviations from the baseline are detected, the system generates an alert or takes predefined actions.

Anomaly-based detection is valuable for identifying zero-day attacks and previously unseen threats that do not have known signatures.

However, it can also generate false positives if the baseline is not accurately calibrated or if legitimate changes in network behavior occur.

To enhance the accuracy of intrusion prevention, advanced strategies often combine both signature-based and anomaly-based techniques.

This hybrid approach provides a more comprehensive view of network activity and can better differentiate between known threats and unusual but legitimate behavior.

Advanced intrusion prevention strategies also prioritize proactive threat intelligence integration.

This involves leveraging threat intelligence feeds and databases that provide real-time information about emerging threats, malicious IP addresses, and vulnerabilities.

By incorporating threat intelligence, IPS can make more informed decisions about blocking or allowing traffic, ensuring that the latest threat information is used to protect the network.

In addition to detecting threats based on signatures or anomalies, advanced intrusion prevention strategies may employ heuristic or behavioral analysis.

Heuristic analysis involves identifying patterns or behaviors that are indicative of malicious activity, even if they do not match known signatures.

Behavioral analysis, on the other hand, focuses on monitoring and analyzing the actions and interactions of network entities, such as users, applications, and devices.

These approaches enable IPS to identify suspicious behavior that may indicate a new or evolving threat.

Furthermore, advanced intrusion prevention strategies incorporate real-time or near-real-time analysis of network traffic and system events.

IPS systems can inspect packets and data streams in real-time, allowing them to block threats as they are detected.

This proactive approach minimizes the potential impact of security incidents and reduces the window of vulnerability.

Advanced intrusion prevention also includes techniques for secure packet inspection and analysis.

This involves deep packet inspection (DPI) to examine the content of data packets, enabling IPS to identify and block malicious payloads or attacks hidden within seemingly innocuous traffic.

For example, DPI can detect and block malicious code embedded within web traffic or email attachments.

Another essential aspect of advanced intrusion prevention is the ability to inspect and protect against threats within encrypted traffic.

As encryption is increasingly used to secure data in transit, attackers may also use encryption to hide their malicious activities.

IPS systems can decrypt and inspect encrypted traffic, ensuring that threats are not concealed within encrypted connections.

This is especially important as many modern threats leverage encrypted protocols.

Intrusion prevention strategies are not limited to the network perimeter; they extend to endpoints, servers, and cloud environments.

Endpoint intrusion prevention solutions protect individual devices, such as desktops, laptops, and mobile devices, from various threats, including malware, ransomware, and advanced persistent threats (APTs).

Server intrusion prevention focuses on safeguarding critical servers and data centers from attacks, while cloud-based IPS solutions protect assets hosted in cloud environments.

Furthermore, advanced intrusion prevention encompasses dynamic security policies that can adapt to changing threat landscapes.

These policies can automatically update and evolve based on real-time threat intelligence, enabling the IPS to respond effectively to emerging threats.

In summary, advanced intrusion prevention strategies combine signature-based and anomaly-based detection methods, threat intelligence integration, heuristic and behavioral analysis, real-time packet inspection, and protection against threats within encrypted traffic.

These strategies proactively defend against a wide range of threats, providing organizations with a robust cybersecurity posture to safeguard their network and data assets.

Chapter 6: Encryption and Data Protection Strategies

Cryptographic algorithms and protocols are foundational elements of modern cybersecurity, providing the means to secure data, communications, and digital identities.

These mathematical techniques play a critical role in protecting information from unauthorized access and ensuring the confidentiality, integrity, and authenticity of data.

At the heart of cryptography are cryptographic algorithms, which are mathematical functions that transform data into a format that is difficult to decipher without the appropriate key.

One of the fundamental types of cryptographic algorithms is symmetric-key encryption, where a single secret key is used for both encryption and decryption.

In symmetric-key encryption, the same key is applied to the plaintext to produce ciphertext, and then the same key is used to reverse the process and recover the original plaintext.

This type of encryption is efficient and well-suited for securing data at rest, such as files and databases.

However, a challenge with symmetric-key encryption is securely distributing and managing the secret key, as both the sender and receiver must possess the same key.

To address this challenge, asymmetric-key encryption, also known as public-key encryption, was developed.

In asymmetric-key encryption, a pair of keys is used: a public key for encryption and a private key for decryption.

The public key can be freely distributed, allowing anyone to encrypt data that only the holder of the corresponding private key can decrypt.

This approach simplifies key management and supports secure communications between parties who have never met before.

One of the most widely used asymmetric encryption algorithms is the RSA algorithm, named after its inventors, Rivest, Shamir, and Adleman.

The RSA algorithm relies on the mathematical properties of large prime numbers, making it computationally difficult to factor the product of two prime numbers to derive the private key from the public key.

Another popular asymmetric encryption algorithm is Elliptic Curve Cryptography (ECC), which offers strong security with shorter key lengths, making it suitable for resource-constrained devices and applications.

Cryptographic protocols define the rules and procedures for using cryptographic algorithms to achieve specific security objectives.

One of the most ubiquitous cryptographic protocols is the Transport Layer Security (TLS) protocol, formerly known as Secure Sockets Layer (SSL).

TLS provides secure communication over the internet, ensuring that data exchanged between a web browser and a web server is encrypted and protected against eavesdropping and tampering.

TLS employs both symmetric and asymmetric encryption to establish a secure channel and authenticate the parties involved.

The protocol also supports forward secrecy, ensuring that even if an attacker obtains the private key in the future, past communications remain secure.

In addition to encryption, cryptographic protocols encompass digital signatures, which are cryptographic techniques that provide authentication and data integrity.

Digital signatures allow a sender to sign a piece of data, such as an email or a software update, using their private key.

The recipient can then verify the signature using the sender's public key, ensuring that the data has not been altered and that it indeed came from the claimed sender.

The Digital Signature Algorithm (DSA) and the Elliptic Curve Digital Signature Algorithm (ECDSA) are commonly used for creating digital signatures.

Cryptographic protocols also include key exchange mechanisms, which allow parties to securely establish shared secret keys over an insecure communication channel.

The Diffie-Hellman key exchange protocol is a well-known example of a key exchange mechanism that enables two parties to generate a shared secret key without exchanging the key directly.

Another key exchange protocol is the Internet Key Exchange (IKE), used in Virtual Private Networks (VPNs) to negotiate secure connections between network devices.

Cryptographic protocols are essential in various applications, such as secure email (PGP/GPG), secure file transfer (SFTP), secure web browsing (HTTPS), and secure instant messaging (Signal).

They are also crucial in securing modern communication technologies, including Voice over IP (VoIP) and Internet of Things (IoT) devices.

However, while cryptographic algorithms and protocols provide strong security, their effectiveness relies on proper implementation and key management practices.

Weaknesses or vulnerabilities in cryptographic software or flawed key management can compromise the security of encrypted data.

Therefore, organizations must stay vigilant in keeping their cryptographic libraries and protocols up to date and following best practices for key generation, storage, and rotation.

In summary, cryptographic algorithms and protocols are the building blocks of modern cybersecurity, enabling the secure transmission and storage of sensitive information.

They encompass symmetric and asymmetric encryption, digital signatures, key exchange mechanisms, and secure communication protocols, all of which play a vital role in safeguarding data and ensuring the trustworthiness of digital communications.

As technology continues to evolve, cryptographic techniques will remain essential in addressing emerging security challenges and protecting the digital world. Data protection beyond encryption encompasses a range of strategies and techniques designed to safeguard sensitive information from unauthorized access and disclosure.

While encryption is a fundamental component of data protection, it is not the sole solution, and additional layers of security are necessary to create a comprehensive defense.

One critical aspect of data protection is access control, which involves defining who can access specific data and what actions they can perform.

Access control mechanisms, such as role-based access control (RBAC) and attribute-based access control (ABAC), allow organizations to enforce fine-grained permissions and restrict access to only authorized users.

Implementing strong authentication methods, including multi-factor authentication (MFA), enhances access control by requiring users to provide multiple forms of verification before accessing sensitive data.

Another essential element of data protection is data classification, where organizations categorize data based on its sensitivity and importance.

This classification informs data handling procedures, ensuring that high-risk data receives the highest level of protection, while less sensitive data may have more relaxed security requirements.

Data loss prevention (DLP) technologies help organizations monitor and prevent the unauthorized movement or sharing of sensitive data, both within and outside the organization.

DLP solutions can identify and block the transfer of confidential information through email, file sharing services, and other communication channels.

Audit and monitoring tools play a crucial role in data protection by continuously tracking data access and usage.

These tools generate logs and alerts for suspicious activities, allowing organizations to detect and respond to potential security incidents promptly.

Additionally, organizations should implement robust data retention and disposal policies.

These policies ensure that data is retained only for as long as necessary and is securely disposed of when it is no longer needed.

Data masking or redaction techniques can be employed to protect sensitive information while allowing the use of data for testing or analysis.

This involves replacing sensitive data with fictional or scrambled values in non-production environments.

Data protection also extends to physical security measures.

Securing data centers and server rooms with access controls, surveillance, and environmental controls prevents unauthorized physical access to servers and storage devices.

Organizations should also establish backup and disaster recovery plans to ensure data availability and integrity in the event of data loss or system failures.

Regularly testing and updating these plans is essential to maintain their effectiveness.

Employee training and awareness programs are essential components of data protection.

Educating staff about security best practices, data handling procedures, and the risks of data breaches can significantly reduce the likelihood of human error leading to data exposure.

Data protection laws and regulations, such as the General Data Protection Regulation (GDPR) and the Health Insurance Portability and Accountability Act (HIPAA), impose legal requirements on organizations to protect personal and sensitive data.

Compliance with these regulations is a crucial aspect of data protection, and failure to do so can result in severe penalties.

In addition to access controls and encryption, data protection strategies also include network security measures.

Firewalls, intrusion detection systems (IDS), and intrusion prevention systems (IPS) help safeguard data by monitoring and controlling network traffic.

Secure web gateways and email filtering solutions can prevent malicious attachments and links from reaching users.

Endpoint security solutions, including antivirus and anti-malware software, protect devices from malicious software that could compromise data.

Application security practices, such as secure coding and vulnerability testing, are essential to prevent data breaches resulting from software vulnerabilities.

Secure coding practices ensure that applications are designed and implemented with security in mind, reducing the risk of exploitation by attackers.

Regular vulnerability testing and penetration testing help organizations identify and remediate potential security weaknesses in their applications and systems.

Data protection also includes securing data in transit.

Virtual Private Networks (VPNs) and secure communication protocols, such as Transport Layer Security (TLS), ensure that data transmitted over networks remains confidential and tamper-proof.

In summary, data protection beyond encryption is a comprehensive approach to safeguarding sensitive information.

It encompasses access control, data classification, data loss prevention, audit and monitoring, data retention and disposal policies, physical security, backup and disaster recovery, employee training, compliance with data protection laws, network security, endpoint security, application security, and secure data transmission.

By implementing a multi-layered approach to data protection, organizations can effectively mitigate the risks of data breaches and ensure the confidentiality, integrity, and availability of their data assets.

Chapter 7: Advanced Access Control and Authentication

Role-Based Access Control (RBAC) is a fundamental security model used in various industries and organizations to manage and enforce access to resources and data.

It provides a structured and efficient approach to access control, allowing organizations to assign permissions and privileges based on job roles and responsibilities.

In RBAC, access permissions are associated with specific roles within an organization rather than with individual users.

This simplifies access management by grouping users with similar responsibilities and access requirements under predefined roles.

RBAC models typically consist of three core elements: roles, permissions, and users.

Roles represent job functions or positions within an organization and define the set of permissions and privileges associated with them.

Permissions are the rules or policies that specify what actions a role or user can perform on specific resources, such as read, write, delete, or execute.

Users are individuals or entities granted access to the system and assigned to one or more roles based on their responsibilities.

One of the key advantages of RBAC is its scalability and ease of administration.

As organizations grow and change, it's often simpler to update role assignments or add new roles to accommodate evolving access requirements.

This flexibility makes RBAC particularly suitable for large enterprises with complex access control needs.

RBAC also enhances security by reducing the risk of granting excessive permissions to users.

With RBAC, access is granted based on roles, ensuring that users can only perform actions required for their specific job functions.

This principle of least privilege minimizes the potential for unauthorized access and helps mitigate security risks.

RBAC can be implemented at various levels, including operating systems, databases, applications, and network devices.

For example, in an operating system, RBAC can be used to define roles such as "system administrator," "database administrator," or "ordinary user."

Each role is associated with specific permissions, such as the ability to create users or modify system settings.

Users are then assigned to roles, allowing them to perform the actions associated with those roles.

RBAC can also be extended to applications, where different user roles have varying levels of access to the application's features and data.

For instance, a customer relationship management (CRM) application might have roles like "sales representative," "sales manager," and "system administrator," each with different permissions.

Implementing RBAC in databases ensures that only authorized users can access, modify, or delete sensitive data. This is crucial for maintaining data integrity and confidentiality, especially in industries with strict data protection requirements, such as healthcare or finance.

Network devices and routers can benefit from RBAC to control who can configure or modify network settings, minimizing the risk of network disruptions or security breaches.

Role-Based Access Control is not a one-size-fits-all solution, and its effectiveness depends on careful planning and implementation.

Organizations need to define roles accurately and determine which permissions should be associated with each role.

Clear documentation of roles and permissions is essential for RBAC to function effectively.

Regular reviews and audits are necessary to ensure that role assignments remain up-to-date and aligned with organizational changes.

RBAC can be extended with the concept of "role hierarchies," where roles inherit permissions from higher-level roles.

This simplifies role management by allowing certain roles to inherit permissions from parent roles while also having their unique permissions.

For example, a "supervisor" role might inherit permissions from a "team leader" role but also have additional permissions specific to supervisors.

Role-Based Access Control can be combined with other security measures, such as Multi-Factor Authentication (MFA) or encryption, to further enhance security.

For example, even if a user has the correct role, they may still need to provide a second factor of authentication to access sensitive data.

In addition to its security benefits, RBAC facilitates compliance with regulatory requirements by ensuring that access to sensitive information is controlled and auditable.

Organizations subject to regulations like the Health Insurance Portability and Accountability Act (HIPAA) or the General Data Protection Regulation (GDPR) can use RBAC to demonstrate that they are managing access to sensitive data responsibly.

However, RBAC is not without its challenges.

One common issue is the potential for role explosion, where the number of roles becomes unwieldy, making administration and auditing complex.

To address this, organizations must strike a balance between granularity and simplicity when defining roles.

Furthermore, RBAC relies on accurate user role assignments, which can be prone to errors.

Organizations must establish clear processes for adding, modifying, or removing users from roles and regularly review role assignments to prevent unauthorized access.

In summary, Role-Based Access Control is a powerful access management model that enhances security, simplifies administration, and supports compliance efforts.

It allows organizations to control access to resources based on job roles and responsibilities, minimizing the risk of unauthorized access and data breaches.

When implemented thoughtfully and maintained diligently, RBAC is a valuable tool for organizations of all sizes and industries.

Multifactor Authentication (MFA) is a robust security method that goes beyond traditional password-based authentication to enhance the protection of digital accounts and systems.

It adds an additional layer of security by requiring users to provide multiple forms of verification before granting access, making it significantly more challenging for unauthorized individuals to gain entry.

The traditional method of authentication, which relies solely on a username and password, has become increasingly vulnerable to cyberattacks.

Password breaches, social engineering, and phishing attacks are common methods used by malicious actors to compromise accounts and systems.

MFA addresses these vulnerabilities by adding one or more additional factors to the authentication process.

These factors typically fall into one of three categories: something you know, something you have, and something you are.

"Something you know" refers to knowledge-based factors, such as a password or a personal identification number (PIN).

"Something you have" involves possession-based factors, such as a smart card, a physical token, or a mobile device.

"Something you are" is based on biometric factors, which include unique physical or behavioral characteristics, like fingerprints, facial recognition, or voice patterns.

By requiring multiple factors from different categories, MFA significantly increases the difficulty of unauthorized access.

One of the most common forms of MFA involves combining a password (something you know) with a temporary code generated by a mobile app or sent via text message (something you have).

To access their accounts, users must first enter their password and then input the time-sensitive code, which is typically valid for a short duration.

Biometric authentication is an increasingly popular and secure form of MFA.

It relies on the unique physical or behavioral traits of individuals to verify their identity.

Fingerprint recognition, for example, scans a person's fingerprint and matches it to stored biometric data to grant access.

Facial recognition technology analyzes facial features and compares them to a database of known faces.

Voice recognition, another biometric method, authenticates users based on their unique voice patterns.

One significant advantage of biometrics is that it is difficult for malicious actors to replicate or steal a person's biometric traits.

However, it's important to note that biometric data must be stored and processed securely to protect individuals' privacy. MFA can be implemented across various systems and applications, including email accounts, online banking, social media, and corporate networks.

Many popular online services, such as Google, Microsoft, and social media platforms, offer MFA options to enhance user account security.

MFA is not only beneficial for individual users but also for organizations looking to secure their networks and data.

In corporate environments, MFA is a crucial component of a robust cybersecurity strategy.

It helps protect sensitive company data, customer information, and intellectual property from unauthorized access and data breaches.

Employees accessing company systems and resources often use MFA to ensure that only authorized personnel can access critical information.

Some organizations go beyond basic MFA and implement adaptive authentication, which uses contextual information to determine the appropriate level of security required for a specific access request.

For example, adaptive authentication might require stronger verification methods if a user attempts to access sensitive data from an unfamiliar location or device.

MFA is not without its challenges.

One common concern is user experience, as the additional verification steps can be perceived as inconvenient.

To mitigate this issue, organizations should select user-friendly MFA methods and provide clear instructions to users.

Another challenge is the potential for MFA methods to be bypassed or compromised.

For example, if a user loses their mobile device with MFA capabilities, an attacker might gain access to their accounts.

To address this, organizations should have protocols in place for reporting lost or stolen devices and should offer alternative methods for authentication.

Furthermore, the effectiveness of MFA relies on the secure management of biometric data or the generation and distribution of temporary codes.

Organizations must implement robust security measures to protect these components of the authentication process.

In summary, Multifactor Authentication (MFA) is a powerful security measure that enhances access control by requiring users to provide multiple forms of verification.

It addresses the vulnerabilities associated with traditional password-based authentication and significantly reduces the risk of unauthorized access.

Biometric authentication, a subset of MFA, offers a secure and convenient way to verify users' identities based on unique physical or behavioral traits.

While MFA is not without challenges, organizations and individuals can benefit greatly from its implementation, providing a stronger defense against cyber threats and data breaches.

Chapter 8: Security Information and Event Management (SIEM)

Security Information and Event Management (SIEM) solutions play a critical role in modern cybersecurity by providing organizations with the capability to monitor, detect, and respond to security incidents and threats.

These solutions serve as the central nervous system of an organization's security infrastructure, collecting and analyzing vast amounts of data from various sources to provide valuable insights into potential security breaches and anomalies.

SIEM architecture typically consists of three main components: data collection, data storage and analysis, and reporting and alerting.

Data collection involves the aggregation of security-related data from a wide range of sources, including network devices, servers, applications, and security tools.

This data is then normalized, meaning it is converted into a consistent format for analysis, allowing for meaningful correlation and detection of security events.

SIEM solutions support various data collection methods, including agents installed on endpoints, network-based data capture, and integration with security appliances and cloud services.

Once the data is collected, it is sent to the data storage and analysis component of the SIEM, often referred to as the SIEM engine.

This component processes the data in real-time or near-real-time, applying correlation rules, threat intelligence, and behavioral analysis to identify potential security incidents.

The SIEM engine uses a combination of predefined rules and user-defined custom rules to detect deviations from normal behavior that may indicate a security threat.

Additionally, it can utilize threat intelligence feeds to identify known malicious indicators, such as IP addresses, domains, and file hashes.

The SIEM engine stores the processed data in a secure and scalable repository, which can be on-premises or in the cloud.

This data serves as a historical record of security events and incidents, enabling forensic analysis, compliance reporting, and long-term trend analysis.

The reporting and alerting component of the SIEM is responsible for generating alerts, reports, and dashboards that provide security teams with actionable insights.

When the SIEM engine detects a security event that meets predefined criteria, it triggers an alert that can be sent to security analysts through various communication channels, such as email, SMS, or a dedicated security console.

These alerts prioritize security incidents based on severity, allowing analysts to focus on the most critical threats first.

In addition to alerts, SIEM solutions offer customizable reporting capabilities that allow organizations to generate compliance reports, executive summaries, and detailed forensic reports for incident investigation and regulatory purposes.

SIEM solutions are instrumental in addressing a wide range of security use cases, including threat detection, incident response, compliance management, and insider threat detection.

One of the primary functions of a SIEM is real-time threat detection.

By continuously monitoring network and system activity, SIEM solutions can identify suspicious behavior that may indicate a security incident, such as unauthorized access attempts, unusual data transfers, or malware activity.

In the event of a security incident, SIEM solutions enable rapid incident response by providing security teams with the necessary context and information to investigate and mitigate threats effectively.

This includes information on the affected systems, the attack vectors, and the timeline of the incident.

SIEM solutions are also valuable for compliance management, as they provide automated reporting capabilities that help organizations demonstrate compliance with various regulatory frameworks and standards, such as the General Data Protection Regulation (GDPR), the Health Insurance Portability and Accountability Act (HIPAA), and the Payment Card Industry Data Security Standard (PCI DSS).

These reports can streamline the audit process and simplify compliance efforts.

Furthermore, SIEM solutions can assist organizations in detecting insider threats by monitoring user behavior and identifying suspicious activities that may indicate malicious intent or data theft.

By correlating user actions with other security events, SIEM solutions can help organizations detect and investigate potential insider threats.

To effectively deploy a SIEM solution, organizations must consider several factors, including the scale of their infrastructure, the complexity of their environment, and their specific security requirements.

The choice between on-premises and cloud-based SIEM solutions depends on an organization's preferences and needs.

On-premises SIEM solutions offer complete control over data and infrastructure but require significant hardware and software investments and ongoing maintenance.

Cloud-based SIEM solutions, on the other hand, provide scalability and ease of deployment but may raise concerns about data privacy and security.

Integration with existing security tools and data sources is essential to ensure that the SIEM solution can collect and analyze relevant data.

Organizations should assess the compatibility of their SIEM solution with their network and security infrastructure, ensuring that it can ingest data from firewalls, intrusion detection systems, antivirus solutions, and other sources.

Another critical aspect of SIEM implementation is the development of effective correlation rules and use cases tailored to an organization's specific threat landscape.

These rules define the criteria for triggering alerts and help focus on the most relevant security events.

Regular tuning and refinement of correlation rules are necessary to reduce false positives and improve the accuracy of threat detection.

Furthermore, organizations should establish incident response processes and workflows that outline the steps to be taken in the event of a security incident.

This includes defining roles and responsibilities, communication procedures, and escalation paths to ensure a coordinated and effective response to threats.

In summary, Security Information and Event Management (SIEM) solutions are indispensable tools in the modern cybersecurity landscape, providing organizations with the ability to monitor, detect, and respond to security incidents and threats effectively.

By collecting and analyzing data from diverse sources, SIEM solutions help identify anomalies and potential security breaches, enabling rapid incident response and compliance management.

Successful SIEM implementation requires careful consideration of factors such as data sources, deployment options, integration with existing tools, and the development of effective correlation rules and incident response procedures.

Real-time security monitoring and analysis are essential components of a proactive cybersecurity strategy that aims to identify and respond to threats as they occur.

In today's digital landscape, where cyber threats are constantly evolving, organizations must be vigilant and employ continuous monitoring to safeguard their networks and data.

Real-time monitoring involves the constant collection and analysis of network and system data to detect unusual or suspicious activities that may indicate security incidents.

By monitoring in real-time, organizations can respond promptly to threats, minimizing potential damage and reducing the impact of security breaches.

One of the primary goals of real-time security monitoring is threat detection, which involves identifying potentially malicious activities or anomalies in the network or system behavior.

This may include monitoring for unauthorized access attempts, unusual traffic patterns, unexpected system modifications, or known indicators of compromise (IoCs) such as malicious IP addresses or file hashes.

To achieve effective real-time monitoring, organizations deploy a variety of security tools and technologies that continuously generate logs and alerts.

These tools can include firewalls, intrusion detection systems (IDS), intrusion prevention systems (IPS), endpoint detection and response (EDR) solutions, and Security Information and Event Management (SIEM) systems.

Logs and alerts generated by these tools are collected and correlated in real-time to provide a comprehensive view of the organization's security posture.

Real-time monitoring is a proactive approach to cybersecurity that enables organizations to identify and respond to threats before they can cause significant damage. In contrast, traditional approaches rely on periodic manual checks and post-incident analysis, which may result in delayed detection and response.

However, real-time monitoring also comes with its own set of challenges and considerations.

One significant challenge is the sheer volume of data generated by various security tools.

The continuous stream of logs and alerts can overwhelm security teams, making it difficult to distinguish between benign events and genuine threats.

To address this challenge, organizations often employ SIEM systems that centralize and automate the collection and correlation of security data.

SIEM systems use predefined rules and machine learning algorithms to sift through the data and prioritize alerts based on their severity and relevance.

Another challenge in real-time monitoring is the need for skilled personnel who can interpret the alerts and take appropriate action.

Security analysts must possess a deep understanding of the organization's network and systems, as well as a knowledge of the latest threats and attack techniques.

To support security analysts, organizations may invest in training and certification programs to ensure they have the skills and knowledge required for effective real-time monitoring.

Furthermore, collaboration and communication among security teams are crucial in a real-time monitoring environment.

When a potential threat is detected, security teams must work together to investigate, contain, and remediate the incident swiftly.

This may involve coordination between network security teams, endpoint security teams, incident response teams, and even external parties such as law enforcement or incident response providers.

The speed and effectiveness of incident response can make a significant difference in mitigating the impact of a security breach.

Real-time monitoring not only detects external threats but also helps organizations identify and address internal risks, including insider threats.

Insider threats can be malicious or unintentional, but both can have serious consequences for an organization.

By monitoring user behavior and access patterns, organizations can identify unusual activities that may indicate insider threats.

This may include employees accessing sensitive data without authorization, attempting to exfiltrate data, or engaging in suspicious activities that deviate from their usual behavior.

Real-time monitoring can also assist organizations in complying with regulatory requirements and industry standards.

Many regulations, such as the General Data Protection Regulation (GDPR) and the Health Insurance Portability and Accountability Act (HIPAA), mandate the continuous monitoring of security events and the timely reporting of data breaches.

Failure to comply with these regulations can result in significant fines and legal repercussions.

To maintain compliance, organizations often leverage real-time monitoring solutions to demonstrate their commitment to data protection and security.

In summary, real-time security monitoring and analysis are vital components of a proactive cybersecurity strategy that enables organizations to detect and respond to threats as they happen.

By continuously monitoring network and system activity, organizations can identify unusual or suspicious behaviors and take immediate action to mitigate risks.

While real-time monitoring comes with its challenges, such as data volume and the need for skilled personnel, it is a crucial defense against evolving cyber threats and helps organizations protect their assets and reputation.

Chapter 9: Threat Hunting and Incident Response

Proactive threat hunting is an essential component of a modern cybersecurity strategy that aims to detect and mitigate threats before they can cause harm.

Unlike reactive approaches that rely on automated security tools and alerts, threat hunting involves a deliberate and systematic search for potential threats within an organization's network and systems.

Proactive threat hunting methodologies are designed to uncover hidden or sophisticated threats that may evade traditional security measures.

One of the fundamental principles of proactive threat hunting is the assumption that determined adversaries can penetrate an organization's defenses.

By adopting this mindset, security teams actively seek out signs of compromise and malicious activities, even when there are no immediate indications of a security breach.

Threat hunting methodologies emphasize the importance of human expertise and intuition in identifying potential threats.

While automated security tools play a crucial role in network defense, they may miss subtle or novel attack techniques that skilled threat hunters can uncover.

Proactive threat hunting involves several key steps and methodologies that security teams can follow to systematically search for threats.

The first step is to define clear objectives and hypotheses for the hunting mission.

Security teams should have a clear understanding of what they are looking for and why.

Hypotheses can be based on threat intelligence, indicators of compromise, or patterns of behavior observed in the organization's environment.

Once the objectives and hypotheses are established, threat hunters collect relevant data from various sources.

This data can include network traffic logs, endpoint logs, firewall logs, and logs from other security devices.

The data collected is then analyzed to identify anomalies, deviations from normal behavior, or potential signs of compromise.

Threat hunters rely on their expertise to distinguish between benign and suspicious activities.

Data analysis can be performed manually or using specialized tools that assist in identifying patterns and anomalies.

During the hunting process, threat hunters may use techniques such as traffic analysis, file analysis, memory analysis, and timeline analysis to piece together the sequence of events and identify potential threats.

Threat hunters also leverage threat intelligence feeds and open-source intelligence to gain insights into known threats and adversary tactics, techniques, and procedures (TTPs).

This knowledge helps them identify indicators of compromise that may be associated with specific threat actors or attack campaigns.

Another important aspect of proactive threat hunting is the use of decoys and honeypots.

Decoys are intentionally exposed assets or networks designed to attract attackers and gather information about their activities.

Honeypots are high-interaction decoys that mimic vulnerable systems and services, luring attackers into a controlled environment where their actions can be closely monitored.

By deploying decoys and honeypots, organizations can gain valuable insights into the tactics and techniques used by threat actors targeting their infrastructure.

Proactive threat hunting is an ongoing process that requires continuous refinement and adaptation.

Security teams should regularly review their hunting methodologies and adjust them based on the evolving threat landscape and the organization's specific needs.

Collaboration and information sharing are essential in proactive threat hunting.

Threat hunters should work closely with incident response teams, threat intelligence analysts, and other security stakeholders to ensure that hunting efforts align with overall security objectives. Additionally, sharing threat hunting findings with the broader cybersecurity community can contribute to collective defense by helping others detect and respond to similar threats.

Proactive threat hunting methodologies should also emphasize the importance of documenting findings and lessons learned. Detailed records of hunting missions, including hypotheses, data sources, analysis techniques, and outcomes, can provide valuable insights for future hunts and contribute to the organization's overall knowledge base.

In summary, proactive threat hunting is a critical component of modern cybersecurity that focuses on actively searching for potential threats within an organization's network and systems. It relies on human expertise, data analysis, and the assumption that determined adversaries can breach defenses. Threat hunters follow systematic methodologies, define clear objectives, and leverage a combination of data sources, analysis techniques, and threat intelligence to uncover hidden or sophisticated threats.

Continuous refinement, collaboration, and documentation are essential elements of effective proactive threat hunting.

Advanced incident response tactics are essential for organizations to effectively detect, contain, and mitigate sophisticated cyber threats that continually evolve in complexity and sophistication.

In today's digital landscape, cyberattacks have become more advanced and persistent, making it crucial for organizations to develop advanced incident response strategies.

These advanced tactics go beyond the basics of incident response and require a deep understanding of cyber threats, adversary techniques, and cutting-edge technology.

One key aspect of advanced incident response is proactive threat hunting, where organizations actively seek out indicators of compromise and signs of malicious activity within their network, even before an incident is detected.

Proactive threat hunting involves analyzing historical data, network traffic, and endpoint activity to identify subtle signs of compromise that may elude automated detection systems.

This approach allows organizations to detect and respond to threats at an earlier stage, reducing the potential impact of a security breach.

Another advanced incident response tactic is leveraging threat intelligence feeds and information-sharing communities to stay informed about the latest threat actors, attack techniques, and vulnerabilities.

By integrating threat intelligence into incident response processes, organizations can prioritize and contextualize alerts, making it easier to identify and respond to high-priority threats.

Furthermore, advanced incident response tactics involve employing deception techniques, such as honeypots and decoy systems, to mislead and deceive attackers.

These decoys mimic legitimate systems and services, diverting attackers' attention away from valuable assets and allowing security teams to monitor attackers' behavior and tactics.

Advanced incident response also requires the use of advanced forensic techniques, including memory analysis and malware reverse engineering.

Memory analysis allows incident responders to examine an endpoint's volatile memory to uncover malicious code, injected processes, or suspicious behavior that may not be visible through traditional disk-based forensics.

Malware reverse engineering involves dissecting malicious code to understand its functionality, capabilities, and potential impact.

This deep analysis helps organizations develop effective countermeasures and prevent similar incidents in the future.

In advanced incident response, the concept of threat intelligence fusion plays a crucial role.

Threat intelligence fusion involves combining multiple sources of threat intelligence, such as open-source intelligence (OSINT), commercial threat feeds, and internally generated threat data, to gain a comprehensive view of the threat landscape.

This integrated approach allows organizations to identify emerging threats and trends, enhancing their incident response capabilities.

Advanced incident response tactics also emphasize the importance of continuous improvement and learning from each incident.

After an incident is resolved, organizations should conduct a thorough post-incident analysis to identify areas for improvement in their security posture, detection capabilities, and response procedures. This process helps organizations adapt and evolve their incident response tactics to stay ahead of evolving threats.

In advanced incident response, organizations must consider the legal and regulatory aspects of incident handling. This includes compliance with data breach notification requirements, privacy regulations, and industry-specific standards.

Understanding the legal implications of an incident and having a well-defined incident response plan that addresses these aspects is crucial for effective response.

Additionally, advanced incident response tactics emphasize the importance of communication and coordination within the organization and with external partners.

Effective communication ensures that all stakeholders are informed and aligned during an incident, from the technical teams working on containment to the executive leadership overseeing the response.

Furthermore, organizations should establish relationships with external partners, such as law enforcement agencies, incident response providers, and legal counsel, to facilitate a coordinated response in the event of a major incident.

In summary, advanced incident response tactics are essential for organizations to effectively combat today's advanced and persistent cyber threats.

These tactics go beyond the basics of incident response and require a proactive approach, threat intelligence integration, deception techniques, advanced forensics, continuous improvement, legal considerations, and effective communication.

By implementing advanced incident response strategies, organizations can enhance their ability to detect, contain, and mitigate sophisticated cyber threats while minimizing the impact of security incidents.

Chapter 10: Achieving Cyber Resilience Excellence

Building a cyber resilience framework is a critical endeavor for organizations in today's digital age, where the threat landscape is constantly evolving, and cyberattacks are becoming increasingly sophisticated.

A cyber resilience framework encompasses a comprehensive set of strategies, processes, and technologies that enable an organization to withstand, adapt to, and recover from cyber threats and incidents.

The concept of cyber resilience goes beyond traditional cybersecurity, focusing on the organization's ability to continue its essential functions and deliver services even in the face of adversity.

A robust cyber resilience framework starts with a clear understanding of the organization's critical assets, data, systems, and processes.

Identifying and prioritizing these assets is crucial for developing effective protection and recovery strategies.

Once the critical assets are identified, organizations can implement a combination of preventive, detective, and corrective measures to safeguard them.

Preventive measures include implementing strong access controls, patching vulnerabilities, and deploying security technologies such as firewalls and antivirus solutions.

Detective measures involve continuous monitoring, threat detection, and incident response capabilities to identify and respond to threats in real-time.

Corrective measures include incident recovery processes, disaster recovery plans, and business continuity strategies to minimize downtime and data loss in the event of a security incident.

One key aspect of building a cyber resilience framework is risk assessment.

Organizations must assess the risks associated with their critical assets and determine the potential impact of cyber threats on their operations.

Risk assessments help organizations prioritize their cybersecurity efforts and allocate resources effectively.

Additionally, organizations should establish clear incident response procedures and a dedicated incident response team.

This team should be well-trained, have defined roles and responsibilities, and follow established incident response playbooks to handle security incidents efficiently.

Moreover, organizations should conduct regular security awareness training for employees to educate them about cybersecurity best practices, the importance of reporting suspicious activities, and their role in the organization's cyber resilience efforts.

Building a cyber resilience framework also involves the implementation of a robust backup and recovery strategy.

Regularly backing up critical data and systems ensures that organizations can quickly recover from a cyber incident and minimize disruption to their operations.

Furthermore, organizations should consider adopting a zero-trust security model, which assumes that no one, whether inside or outside the network, can be trusted by default.

Zero-trust principles include strict access controls, continuous monitoring, and the principle of "never trust, always verify."

By implementing a zero-trust approach, organizations can reduce the attack surface and enhance their cyber resilience.

Another important component of a cyber resilience framework is threat intelligence.

Organizations should continuously monitor the threat landscape, gather intelligence on emerging threats, and stay informed about adversary tactics and techniques.

Threat intelligence feeds and services can provide valuable insights to help organizations proactively defend against cyber threats.

Additionally, organizations should consider conducting regular penetration testing and vulnerability assessments to identify and address weaknesses in their security posture.

These assessments help organizations identify vulnerabilities that attackers may exploit and take proactive measures to mitigate these risks.

Building a cyber resilience framework is an ongoing process that requires continuous improvement and adaptation.

Organizations should regularly review and update their cybersecurity policies, procedures, and technologies to address new threats and challenges.

They should also conduct tabletop exercises and simulations to test their incident response plans and assess their readiness to handle security incidents effectively.

Furthermore, organizations should establish relationships with external partners, such as incident response providers, law enforcement agencies, and industry-specific organizations, to facilitate a coordinated response in the event of a major cyber incident.

In summary, building a cyber resilience framework is essential for organizations to protect their critical assets and operations in the face of evolving cyber threats.

This framework encompasses risk assessment, preventive, detective, and corrective measures, incident response capabilities, security awareness, backup and recovery strategies, zero-trust principles, threat intelligence, and continuous improvement.

By implementing a robust cyber resilience framework, organizations can enhance their ability to withstand and recover from cyber incidents, ensuring the continuity of their essential functions and services.

Continual improvement in cyber resilience is a fundamental principle for organizations looking to enhance their ability to withstand and recover from cyber threats and incidents.
Cyber resilience is not a static state; it's an ongoing process that requires constant vigilance, adaptation, and refinement.
One of the key aspects of continual improvement in cyber resilience is the regular assessment of an organization's cybersecurity posture.
This involves conducting comprehensive security assessments and audits to identify vulnerabilities, weaknesses, and areas that need improvement.
By regularly assessing their security posture, organizations can stay informed about their current risk levels and take proactive measures to address vulnerabilities.
Moreover, organizations should conduct post-incident reviews and analyses after every cybersecurity incident.
These reviews should examine the incident response process, identify areas for improvement, and capture lessons learned.
By analyzing incidents and their root causes, organizations can refine their incident response procedures, enhance their detection capabilities, and prevent similar incidents in the future.
Continual improvement in cyber resilience also entails the continuous monitoring of the threat landscape.
Cyber threats are constantly evolving, and new attack techniques emerge regularly.
Organizations must stay informed about the latest threats and vulnerabilities by monitoring threat intelligence feeds,

participating in information-sharing communities, and following cybersecurity news.

This awareness allows organizations to adapt their defenses and strategies to address emerging threats effectively.

Another important aspect of continual improvement in cyber resilience is the development and implementation of a robust cybersecurity training and awareness program for employees.

Regularly educating and training employees on cybersecurity best practices helps create a culture of security within the organization.

Employees become more vigilant about potential threats, better equipped to recognize phishing attempts, and more aware of their role in protecting the organization's digital assets.

Furthermore, organizations should establish clear incident response playbooks and procedures.

These playbooks should be regularly reviewed and updated to align with the evolving threat landscape and the organization's specific needs.

Testing and simulating various incident scenarios through tabletop exercises help ensure that incident response teams are well-prepared and can effectively handle security incidents.

Continual improvement also involves the development of a proactive threat hunting program.

Threat hunters actively seek out indicators of compromise and signs of malicious activity within an organization's network.

By proactively hunting for threats, organizations can detect and mitigate threats at an early stage, reducing the potential impact of a security breach.

Additionally, organizations should regularly update and patch their systems and software to address known vulnerabilities.

Cybercriminals often exploit known weaknesses, so keeping systems up to date is essential for reducing the attack surface.

Regular patch management helps protect against common attack vectors.

Moreover, organizations should consider the implementation of a Security Information and Event Management (SIEM) system.

SIEM systems collect, analyze, and correlate security data from various sources to identify potential threats.

These systems provide real-time insights into security incidents and enable organizations to respond promptly.

Furthermore, organizations should engage in threat intelligence sharing and collaboration with other entities in their industry or sector.

Sharing threat intelligence helps organizations collectively defend against common threats and provides a broader context for understanding the threat landscape.

Another aspect of continual improvement in cyber resilience is establishing key performance indicators (KPIs) and metrics to measure the effectiveness of cybersecurity efforts.

Organizations can track these KPIs to assess their progress in achieving cyber resilience goals and identify areas that require further attention.

Furthermore, organizations should conduct regular security drills and simulations to test their incident response plans and validate their cybersecurity measures.

These drills help incident response teams practice their roles, refine their procedures, and ensure that they can effectively manage security incidents.

In summary, continual improvement in cyber resilience is vital for organizations to adapt and thrive in an ever-changing cybersecurity landscape.

This process involves regular security assessments, post-incident reviews, threat monitoring, employee training, incident response playbook development, threat hunting, patch management, SIEM implementation, threat intelligence sharing, KPI tracking, and security drills.

By embracing a culture of continual improvement, organizations can enhance their cyber resilience and better protect their digital assets and operations.

BOOK 4
DEFENSE IN DEPTH MASTERY
EXPERT-LEVEL TECHNIQUES FOR UNPARALLELED CYBER
RESILIENCE IN NETWORK SECURITY

ROB BOTWRIGHT

Chapter 1: The Evolving Landscape of Cyber Threats

In the rapidly evolving landscape of cybersecurity, modern threat vectors and attack techniques have become increasingly sophisticated and pervasive.

These threats are a growing concern for organizations of all sizes, from small businesses to large enterprises.

One of the prevalent modern threat vectors is phishing, which involves attackers impersonating legitimate entities to trick individuals into revealing sensitive information such as passwords or financial details.

Phishing attacks have evolved beyond simple email campaigns and now include more advanced variants like spear-phishing, where attackers tailor their messages to specific targets.

Another modern threat vector is ransomware, which encrypts an organization's data and demands a ransom for its decryption.

Ransomware attacks often target critical infrastructure and can cause severe disruption and financial loss.

To evade detection, ransomware operators are continuously refining their techniques.

A concerning trend in recent years is the rise of nation-state-sponsored cyberattacks.

These attacks are often highly sophisticated and can target governments, critical infrastructure, or private organizations.

Nation-state actors have advanced capabilities and resources, making their attacks particularly challenging to defend against.

Moreover, supply chain attacks have gained prominence, where attackers compromise software or hardware suppliers to infiltrate their target organizations.

These attacks can have far-reaching consequences and pose a significant threat to supply chain integrity.

In addition to traditional malware, attackers are increasingly using fileless malware, which operates in memory and leaves no trace on disk, making it harder to detect.

Fileless malware leverages legitimate system tools to carry out malicious activities, making it a potent threat vector.

The Internet of Things (IoT) has introduced a new set of security challenges, with attackers targeting vulnerable IoT devices to gain access to networks.

Weak security practices and outdated firmware make IoT devices attractive targets for attackers seeking to exploit them as entry points.

Moreover, credential stuffing attacks are on the rise, where attackers use stolen usernames and passwords from one breach to gain unauthorized access to multiple accounts across different platforms.

These attacks are made possible by individuals reusing passwords across various online services.

Social engineering remains a potent attack technique, with attackers manipulating human psychology to gain access to sensitive information.

Attackers may use social engineering in conjunction with other threat vectors, such as phishing or pretexting.

Advanced persistent threats (APTs) are another modern threat vector, where attackers maintain a persistent presence within a network, often for an extended period.

APTs are typically orchestrated by well-funded and organized threat actors with specific objectives.

In recent years, attacks targeting cloud infrastructure and services have become prevalent.

As organizations increasingly move their data and operations to the cloud, attackers are adapting their strategies to exploit vulnerabilities in cloud environments.

Zero-day vulnerabilities, which are unknown to the vendor and have no available patches, pose a significant threat.

Attackers may discover and exploit these vulnerabilities before security teams can implement mitigations.

Furthermore, insider threats, whether intentional or unintentional, continue to be a concern.

Malicious insiders with access to an organization's systems and data can cause significant harm, while unintentional insider actions can lead to data breaches.

To counter these modern threat vectors and attack techniques, organizations must adopt a multi-layered security approach.

This includes robust email filtering and security awareness training to combat phishing attacks.

Effective backup and recovery strategies are crucial for mitigating the impact of ransomware attacks.

Advanced endpoint protection solutions can help detect and prevent fileless malware.

IoT devices should be securely configured, and network segmentation can isolate them from critical systems.

Implementing strong password policies and multi-factor authentication can thwart credential stuffing attacks.

Employee training and awareness programs are essential to recognize and resist social engineering attempts.

To defend against APTs, organizations should focus on continuous monitoring and threat hunting.

Securing cloud environments requires proper configuration, monitoring, and access control.

Vulnerability management is crucial for addressing zero-day vulnerabilities.

Monitoring user activities and implementing access controls can help mitigate insider threats.

In summary, understanding modern threat vectors and attack techniques is essential for organizations to effectively protect their digital assets and sensitive data.

These threats are dynamic and constantly evolving, requiring organizations to adopt proactive and adaptive security measures to defend against them.

By staying informed about the latest threat trends and investing in robust cybersecurity practices, organizations can better safeguard their digital environments and maintain cyber resilience in the face of modern threats.

In the age of IoT (Internet of Things) and AI (Artificial Intelligence), the cybersecurity landscape has undergone a significant transformation, introducing new dimensions to cyber threats and challenges.

IoT devices, ranging from smart appliances to industrial sensors, have become ubiquitous in our daily lives and critical in various industries, but they also present a host of security vulnerabilities.

These devices are often designed with limited computing resources, making them susceptible to attacks due to weak security measures and outdated firmware.

One of the primary concerns with IoT devices is their susceptibility to botnet attacks, where a large number of compromised devices are controlled by attackers to carry out malicious activities, such as Distributed Denial of Service (DDoS) attacks.

The proliferation of IoT devices has expanded the attack surface, providing cybercriminals with more entry points into networks.

Additionally, IoT devices often lack robust security mechanisms, making them easy targets for exploitation.

The interconnected nature of IoT ecosystems amplifies the potential impact of security breaches.

AI technologies, on the other hand, have introduced both new opportunities and challenges in the realm of cybersecurity.

AI-powered systems are increasingly being used by organizations for threat detection, anomaly detection, and automated response.

However, cybercriminals are also harnessing AI to create more sophisticated and evasive attacks.

AI-driven attacks can adapt in real-time, making them challenging to detect and mitigate.

One such example is the use of AI-generated deepfake content, where attackers manipulate audio or video to impersonate individuals or organizations for malicious purposes.

Deepfake attacks can undermine trust and credibility, leading to various social engineering and phishing schemes.

Furthermore, AI can be used to enhance the effectiveness of phishing attacks by creating highly convincing and personalized messages that are difficult for individuals to discern as fraudulent.

The use of AI in social engineering attacks has the potential to significantly increase the success rate of these campaigns.

Another emerging threat is AI-enhanced malware, where machine learning algorithms are used to develop malware that can adapt and evolve to evade traditional cybersecurity defenses.

These AI-powered malware variants can quickly identify and exploit vulnerabilities, making them highly effective and challenging to combat.

In the age of IoT and AI, the security of critical infrastructure has become a paramount concern.

Many essential services, such as energy grids, transportation systems, and healthcare facilities, rely on interconnected IoT devices and AI-driven systems.

A successful cyberattack on these systems can have dire consequences, ranging from service disruptions to public safety risks.

Moreover, the integration of AI into critical infrastructure introduces the potential for AI-driven attacks that could manipulate automated systems or disrupt their functionality.

To address the evolving cyber threats in the age of IoT and AI, organizations must adopt a proactive and multi-layered cybersecurity approach.

This approach includes robust network segmentation to isolate IoT devices and critical systems from less secure parts of the network.

IoT device manufacturers need to prioritize security in their designs, including regular firmware updates and secure-by-design principles.

Furthermore, organizations should invest in AI-driven cybersecurity solutions that can analyze vast amounts of data to detect anomalies and threats in real-time.

Machine learning and AI can help identify patterns indicative of attacks and provide rapid response capabilities.

Additionally, cybersecurity professionals need to stay abreast of the latest AI-driven attack techniques and continuously update their defenses to adapt to evolving threats.

Regular training and awareness programs for employees are crucial to educate them about the risks associated with IoT and AI-driven attacks.

Furthermore, robust incident response plans and disaster recovery strategies are essential for minimizing the impact of successful cyberattacks.

Collaboration among governments, organizations, and the technology industry is crucial to developing cybersecurity standards and regulations that address the unique challenges posed by IoT and AI.

In summary, the age of IoT and AI has ushered in new and complex cybersecurity threats that require innovative and adaptive defenses.

As technology continues to advance, organizations must remain vigilant and proactive in their efforts to secure their digital ecosystems and protect critical infrastructure.

By understanding the evolving threat landscape and investing in cybersecurity measures that leverage AI and other advanced technologies, organizations can better defend against the multifaceted challenges posed by IoT and AI-driven cyber threats.

Chapter 2: Advanced Network Architecture and Topologies

In the realm of network security, scalable designs play a pivotal role in ensuring that security measures can adapt and expand to meet the evolving needs of organizations.

Scalability is a critical consideration because networks must be able to accommodate growth in data traffic, devices, and users while maintaining robust security.

A scalable network design allows for seamless expansion without compromising security integrity.

One fundamental aspect of scalable network designs is the consideration of network segmentation.

Segmentation involves dividing the network into smaller, isolated segments or zones, each with its own security policies and access controls.

This segmentation strategy enhances security by limiting the lateral movement of threats within the network.

Moreover, it allows organizations to scale their security measures effectively by applying specific controls to different network segments.

One common segmentation approach is the creation of Virtual LANs (VLANs), which enable the isolation of devices and users into logical groups.

Each VLAN can have its own security policies, reducing the attack surface and preventing unauthorized access to sensitive resources.

Scalable network designs also incorporate the principle of defense in depth, which involves layering multiple security measures to protect against various threats.

This approach recognizes that no single security measure is foolproof, and a combination of defenses provides a more robust security posture.

By layering security controls such as firewalls, intrusion detection systems, and access controls, organizations can better mitigate risks and adapt to changing threat landscapes.

Furthermore, scalable network designs take into account the dynamic nature of modern IT environments.

Cloud adoption, remote work, and the proliferation of mobile devices have created a more fluid network ecosystem.

To address these challenges, scalable designs embrace flexibility and adaptability.

They allow for the integration of cloud security solutions and provide secure access for remote users and devices.

Scalability extends beyond traditional network boundaries and encompasses the ability to expand security measures to new technology trends.

The Internet of Things (IoT), for instance, introduces a wide range of interconnected devices into networks.

A scalable network design should accommodate IoT security by enforcing strict access controls, monitoring device behavior, and segmenting IoT devices from critical network resources.

Furthermore, as organizations increasingly rely on hybrid and multi-cloud environments, scalable network designs must incorporate cloud-native security solutions.

These solutions leverage automation and orchestration to scale security measures in tandem with cloud resources.

Scalable network designs also consider the importance of threat intelligence in enhancing security.

By incorporating threat feeds and analysis, organizations can proactively adapt their security measures to counter emerging threats.

Threat intelligence helps identify indicators of compromise and provides valuable context for security decision-making.

Moreover, scalability in network designs means having the ability to implement continuous monitoring and analysis.

Network traffic analysis and anomaly detection play a crucial role in identifying and responding to security incidents.

Scalable designs enable the deployment of security information and event management (SIEM) systems and security analytics tools to monitor network behavior for potential threats.

Additionally, scalability encompasses the automation of security processes.

By automating routine tasks such as patch management, access provisioning, and incident response, organizations can scale their security operations efficiently.

Automation reduces the burden on security teams and accelerates incident detection and response.

Another facet of scalability in network designs involves the integration of zero-trust security principles.

Zero-trust assumes that no entity, whether inside or outside the network, can be trusted by default.

Instead, it enforces strict access controls and authentication mechanisms, even within the network perimeter.

Scalable designs facilitate the adoption of zero-trust by allowing organizations to implement micro-segmentation and user-specific access controls.

Scalable network designs are not static but evolve in response to changing security threats and organizational needs.

They incorporate the concept of continuous improvement, where security measures are regularly assessed and adjusted.

Scalability ensures that as networks grow and technology evolves, security measures can adapt without requiring a complete overhaul of the infrastructure.

In summary, scalable network designs are foundational to modern network security.

They enable organizations to adapt to the ever-changing threat landscape, accommodate growth, and embrace new technologies while maintaining robust security postures.

By embracing segmentation, defense in depth, flexibility, threat intelligence, continuous monitoring, automation, and zero-trust principles, organizations can build network infrastructures that are both secure and adaptable to the challenges of the digital age.

In the realm of network architecture and design, the pursuit of advanced topologies has become essential to achieving both resilience and performance in modern networks.

These advanced topologies go beyond the traditional network layouts to address the demands of today's digital landscape.

One such advanced topology is the use of redundant, fault-tolerant designs that ensure network availability even in the face of hardware failures or disruptions.

Redundancy involves duplicating critical network components, such as switches, routers, and links, to create backup paths for data traffic.

This redundancy mitigates single points of failure and enhances network resilience.

In high-availability designs, failover mechanisms are employed to automatically switch to redundant components in case of a failure, minimizing downtime.

Another advanced topology that enhances network performance is the use of load balancing.

Load balancers distribute network traffic across multiple servers or network paths to ensure optimal resource utilization and prevent overload on individual components.

Load balancing is particularly valuable in data center environments, where large volumes of traffic must be efficiently managed.

By distributing workloads evenly, load balancers improve response times and minimize the risk of service degradation.

Furthermore, advanced network topologies incorporate the concept of hierarchical design, which organizes the network into distinct layers.

Hierarchical design simplifies network management and enhances scalability.

The core layer provides high-speed, high-capacity connectivity, while the distribution layer handles routing and traffic filtering.

At the access layer, devices such as switches connect end-users and devices to the network.

Hierarchical design promotes efficient traffic flow and isolates network changes within specific layers, reducing the impact of changes on the entire network.

In addition to redundancy, advanced topologies also embrace diversity in network paths.

Diverse paths involve utilizing different physical routes for network traffic, often achieved through multiple carriers or Internet Service Providers (ISPs).

Diversity enhances resilience by reducing the risk of a single point of failure due to a carrier outage or network disruption.

It also provides an added layer of security against certain types of attacks.

Furthermore, advanced topologies incorporate the concept of scalability, which ensures that the network can grow to accommodate increased demands without significant redesign.

Scalable designs often use modular components that can be easily added or expanded as needed.

This adaptability is crucial in today's dynamic digital environments, where businesses experience rapid growth or fluctuations in demand.

Software-Defined Networking (SDN) is another advanced topology that has gained prominence in recent years.

SDN decouples network control and data forwarding, allowing for centralized management and programmable network configurations.

This flexibility enhances network agility and enables the automation of tasks, reducing operational overhead.

Furthermore, SDN can optimize network traffic based on real-time demands, improving performance and resource utilization.

Advanced topologies also consider the importance of security in network design.

Security measures are integrated into the design to protect against threats and vulnerabilities.

For example, the use of segmented networks, where different parts of the network are isolated from each other, limits the lateral movement of attackers and reduces the impact of breaches.

Moreover, security policies and access controls are enforced at various network levels to prevent unauthorized access and data breaches.

Another advanced topology is the use of virtualization and cloud integration.

Virtual networks and cloud-based services enable organizations to scale resources dynamically, optimizing performance and cost-efficiency.

They also provide the flexibility to extend network services beyond the traditional boundaries of physical infrastructure.

Furthermore, advanced topologies consider the importance of quality of service (QoS) mechanisms.

QoS ensures that critical applications receive priority treatment, guaranteeing that they meet performance requirements.

By prioritizing traffic based on application needs, organizations can enhance the user experience and maintain efficient network operations.

Additionally, advanced topologies leverage advanced routing protocols and algorithms to optimize data traffic.

These protocols consider factors such as latency, bandwidth availability, and network congestion to determine the most efficient path for data transmission.

Dynamic routing protocols can adapt to network changes in real-time, ensuring that data is routed along the best path at all times.

In summary, advanced network topologies are essential components of modern network architecture.

They provide the foundation for resilient, high-performance networks that can adapt to the demands of today's digital world.

By embracing redundancy, load balancing, hierarchical design, diversity, scalability, SDN, security measures, virtualization, cloud integration, QoS, and advanced routing protocols, organizations can build networks that excel in both reliability and performance.

Chapter 3: Threat Intelligence and Cyber Espionage

In the ever-evolving landscape of cybersecurity, the gathering and utilization of threat intelligence have become integral components of an effective defense strategy.

Threat intelligence encompasses a wide range of information related to potential and existing threats that could target an organization's network and data.

This information includes details about the tactics, techniques, and procedures (TTPs) employed by threat actors, as well as indicators of compromise (IOCs) that may signal a security incident.

Effective threat intelligence can provide organizations with valuable insights into the nature and scope of cyber threats, enabling proactive defense measures.

One of the primary sources of threat intelligence is open-source intelligence (OSINT), which involves collecting information from publicly available sources, including websites, forums, social media, and news articles.

OSINT can provide early indications of emerging threats, such as new vulnerabilities, attack trends, or hacker activities.

Another source of threat intelligence is commercial threat feeds, which are curated databases of threat data that organizations can subscribe to.

These feeds aggregate information from a variety of sources, including security vendors, government agencies, and industry-specific organizations.

Commercial threat feeds offer a more structured and comprehensive source of threat intelligence, often providing real-time updates on known threats and vulnerabilities.

Furthermore, organizations can contribute to threat intelligence sharing initiatives, where they share information about their own security incidents and experiences with trusted partners or industry-specific Information Sharing and Analysis Centers (ISACs).

This collective sharing of threat data helps create a broader and more detailed picture of the threat landscape.

Once organizations have access to threat intelligence, they must analyze and contextualize the information to make it actionable.

This process involves understanding the relevance of the intelligence to the organization's specific environment and risk profile.

Not all threats are equally applicable or impactful to every organization, so context is essential in prioritizing and addressing the most relevant threats.

Threat intelligence analysis often includes identifying patterns and trends within the data to anticipate potential future threats.

It may also involve correlating threat data with the organization's own network and security logs to identify any matches or anomalies.

Once threat intelligence has been analyzed and contextualized, organizations can use it to inform their security strategies and decision-making.

For example, if a specific type of malware is trending in threat intelligence reports, an organization can proactively update its antivirus and intrusion detection systems to detect and block that malware.

Threat intelligence can also inform vulnerability management programs, helping organizations prioritize patching and remediation efforts based on the most critical vulnerabilities being actively exploited in the wild.

Furthermore, threat intelligence can be used to enhance incident response capabilities.

By pre-emptively identifying indicators of compromise associated with known threats, organizations can reduce the time it takes to detect and respond to security incidents.

Additionally, threat intelligence can be integrated into security awareness and training programs to educate employees about emerging threats and phishing campaigns.

Automation plays a crucial role in the effective utilization of threat intelligence.

Organizations can automate the ingestion of threat data from various sources and use it to automatically update security controls and policies.

For example, if a threat intelligence feed reports a surge in Distributed Denial of Service (DDoS) attacks originating from a specific region, an organization can automatically adjust its firewall rules to block traffic from that region.

Automation enables organizations to respond rapidly to emerging threats, reducing the window of vulnerability.

Moreover, threat intelligence can be used to enhance threat hunting activities.

Threat hunters proactively search for signs of malicious activity within an organization's network.

By leveraging threat intelligence, they can focus their efforts on specific indicators and TTPs associated with known threats, improving the efficiency and effectiveness of their hunting efforts.

It's important to note that the threat landscape is constantly evolving, and threat intelligence is not a static resource.

Organizations must continuously update and refine their threat intelligence sources and analysis techniques to stay ahead of emerging threats.

Additionally, sharing threat intelligence with trusted partners and industry peers fosters a collaborative defense approach that benefits the entire cybersecurity community.

In summary, gathering and utilizing threat intelligence is a critical aspect of modern cybersecurity.

It provides organizations with valuable insights into emerging threats and vulnerabilities, enabling them to proactively defend against cyberattacks.

Whether through OSINT, commercial threat feeds, or collaborative sharing initiatives, threat intelligence empowers organizations to make informed decisions, automate security measures, enhance incident response, and ultimately strengthen their overall security posture.

In the world of cybersecurity, advanced techniques in cyber espionage represent a significant and growing threat to governments, organizations, and individuals alike.

Cyber espionage refers to the covert and often targeted theft of sensitive information or intelligence from a victim's computer systems or networks.

Unlike cybercrime, which seeks financial gain or disruption, cyber espionage is motivated by the desire to access classified or confidential data for espionage, political, or military purposes.

This form of digital espionage has become increasingly sophisticated and prevalent in recent years, posing a substantial challenge to defenders.

One of the key characteristics of advanced cyber espionage techniques is the use of tailored or custom malware, often referred to as Advanced Persistent Threats (APTs).

APTs are designed to remain undetected within a target's network for extended periods, allowing threat actors to gather intelligence or conduct surveillance over an extended period.

These APTs are typically developed by well-funded and organized state-sponsored groups, criminal organizations, or hacktivists with specific objectives in mind.

To evade detection, APTs are often delivered through spear-phishing emails or malicious websites that exploit unpatched vulnerabilities in the victim's software.

Once inside the target's network, APTs employ various evasion tactics, such as living off the land (LOL) techniques, which involve using legitimate system utilities and tools to blend in with normal network traffic.

This makes it challenging for security teams to identify and isolate the malicious activity.

Another advanced technique used in cyber espionage is the exploitation of zero-day vulnerabilities.

Zero-day vulnerabilities are software flaws that are unknown to the software vendor and, therefore, have no available patches or fixes.

Threat actors who discover these vulnerabilities can use them to gain unauthorized access to systems and conduct espionage activities.

To protect against this threat, organizations and governments invest heavily in vulnerability research and security patching.

Furthermore, advanced cyber espionage techniques often involve the use of rootkits and kernel-level malware, which can manipulate the operating system's core functions to conceal their presence.

These techniques make it extremely difficult for security software to detect and remove the malicious code.

Rootkits are particularly effective in achieving persistence within a compromised system, as they can reinstall themselves even after removal attempts.

Advanced cyber espionage actors also engage in "watering hole" attacks, where they compromise websites frequented by their target audience.

When victims visit these compromised websites, their devices can be infected with malware, enabling attackers to gain access to their systems.

This approach leverages trust in well-known websites to carry out espionage activities.

Moreover, advanced cyber espionage campaigns often involve multi-stage attacks, where initial compromises serve as a foothold for further infiltration.

Threat actors move laterally within a target's network, progressively escalating privileges and exfiltrating sensitive data.

This approach allows attackers to access high-value targets, such as classified information or proprietary research.

Furthermore, advanced cyber espionage techniques include the use of sophisticated command-and-control (C2) infrastructure.

C2 servers are used by threat actors to communicate with compromised systems, issue commands, and exfiltrate stolen data.

These C2 servers are designed to be resilient and difficult to trace, often relying on proxy networks or encryption to conceal their true location.

In some cases, advanced cyber espionage actors use compromised infrastructure belonging to legitimate organizations to host their C2 servers, making attribution even more challenging.

To combat these advanced techniques, organizations and governments invest in cutting-edge cybersecurity measures.

These measures include advanced threat detection systems that employ machine learning and behavioral analytics to identify unusual patterns of activity indicative of espionage.

Security teams also engage in threat hunting, actively seeking out indicators of compromise and APT activity within their networks.

Moreover, organizations and governments engage in threat intelligence sharing to stay informed about emerging cyber threats and attack techniques.

Collaborative efforts among security professionals and the sharing of threat data help in the early detection and mitigation of cyber espionage campaigns.

Advanced techniques in cyber espionage pose a formidable challenge to defenders, requiring constant vigilance, sophisticated security measures, and collaboration within the cybersecurity community.

As the digital landscape continues to evolve, cyber espionage actors will undoubtedly develop even more advanced tactics, making it imperative for organizations and governments to adapt and strengthen their defenses continually.

Chapter 4: Advanced Firewall Customization and Optimization

In the realm of network security, the fine-tuning of firewall rules and policies plays a critical role in safeguarding an organization's digital assets and data.

Firewalls serve as the first line of defense against cyber threats, filtering incoming and outgoing network traffic based on a set of predefined rules and policies.

These rules and policies determine which traffic is allowed to pass through the firewall and which is blocked, forming a crucial barrier that helps prevent unauthorized access and potential security breaches.

To maximize the effectiveness of a firewall, organizations must engage in a continuous process of refining and fine-tuning their rules and policies to adapt to evolving threats and network requirements.

One of the initial steps in fine-tuning firewall rules is the establishment of a clear and well-documented security policy.

This policy outlines the organization's security objectives, defines acceptable use of the network, and specifies the types of traffic that should be allowed or denied.

A comprehensive security policy serves as the foundation upon which firewall rules and policies are built.

When crafting firewall rules, organizations often use a default-deny approach, meaning that all traffic is denied by default unless explicitly allowed by a rule.

This approach minimizes the attack surface and ensures that only necessary and trusted traffic is permitted.

As part of the fine-tuning process, organizations regularly review and update their firewall rulesets.

This involves removing outdated rules, consolidating overlapping rules, and adding new rules as needed to accommodate changes in network infrastructure or security requirements.

In some cases, organizations may perform a rule audit to identify and eliminate rules that are no longer relevant or effective.

Another crucial aspect of fine-tuning firewall rules is ensuring that rules are granular and specific, rather than overly permissive.

Granular rules allow organizations to precisely control traffic based on criteria such as source and destination IP addresses, port numbers, and protocols.

Overly permissive rules, on the other hand, can inadvertently expose the network to security risks by allowing unnecessary traffic.

To strike the right balance between security and functionality, organizations often implement stateful firewall inspection.

Stateful inspection involves tracking the state of active connections and allowing only valid responses to outbound traffic.

This ensures that only traffic associated with established connections is permitted, while other potentially malicious traffic is blocked.

Fine-tuning firewall rules also entails considering the principle of least privilege.

This means that rules should only grant access to the resources and services necessary for legitimate business operations.

Unnecessary access should be restricted, reducing the attack surface and limiting potential security vulnerabilities.

Organizations should regularly monitor firewall logs and alerts to identify any anomalies or suspicious activity.

Log analysis can help uncover unauthorized access attempts, unusual traffic patterns, or signs of a potential breach.

Fine-tuning firewall rules based on log data and incident response procedures can help organizations respond quickly to security incidents and mitigate potential damage.

Furthermore, organizations often segment their networks into zones and implement firewall rules to control traffic flow between these zones.

For example, a demilitarized zone (DMZ) might be established to host public-facing services, with strict rules governing traffic between the DMZ and internal network segments.

Fine-tuning these zone-based rules ensures that network segments are appropriately isolated, preventing lateral movement by attackers.

In addition to network segmentation, organizations may also apply firewall rules at the application layer to control access to specific applications or services.

Application layer firewalls inspect and filter traffic based on application-layer protocols and content.

This allows organizations to enforce policies that dictate how applications are used within the network, preventing unauthorized or malicious use.

Fine-tuning application layer firewall rules involves creating rules that align with the organization's application usage policies and ensuring that they are regularly reviewed and updated. Moreover, fine-tuning firewall rules often includes the use of intrusion detection and prevention system (IDPS) integration.

IDPS solutions work in conjunction with firewalls to identify and block known attack patterns and signatures. Fine-tuning rules that govern IDPS integration helps organizations stay current with emerging threats and ensures that their security controls are effective in detecting and preventing attacks.

Firewall rule optimization is an ongoing process, as the threat landscape and network environment are constantly evolving. Organizations must stay informed about emerging threats and vulnerabilities and adjust their firewall rules accordingly.

Collaboration with industry peers and sharing threat intelligence can be invaluable in this regard. In summary, fine-tuning firewall rules and policies is an essential element of effective network security.

It involves establishing clear security policies, regularly reviewing and updating rulesets, implementing granular and specific rules, monitoring logs, segmenting networks, and integrating with IDPS solutions.

By continually optimizing firewall rules, organizations can maintain a strong defense against cyber threats and adapt to the ever-changing cybersecurity landscape.

In the realm of cybersecurity, optimizing firewall performance is a critical aspect of maintaining robust network security.

Firewalls are a fundamental component of any organization's security infrastructure, serving as the gatekeepers that control the flow of network traffic and protect against malicious threats.

However, for firewalls to effectively safeguard an organization's digital assets and data, their performance must be optimized to strike the right balance between security and functionality.

To achieve this balance, organizations must take several factors into consideration when optimizing their firewall performance.

One of the key factors in firewall optimization is selecting the appropriate type of firewall for the organization's specific needs.

There are different types of firewalls available, including stateful inspection firewalls, proxy firewalls, and application-layer firewalls, each with its own strengths and weaknesses.

Choosing the right type of firewall depends on factors such as the organization's network architecture, security requirements, and the types of threats it needs to defend against.

Once the appropriate firewall type is selected, organizations need to ensure that the firewall hardware and software are up to date and capable of handling the network traffic volume.

Outdated or insufficient hardware can lead to performance bottlenecks, resulting in slow network speeds and reduced security efficacy.

Regular hardware upgrades and software updates are essential to maintain optimal firewall performance.

Another critical aspect of firewall optimization is the fine-tuning of firewall rules and policies.

Firewalls rely on rules to determine which traffic is allowed or denied based on predefined criteria such as source and destination IP addresses, port numbers, and protocols.

To optimize firewall performance, organizations must regularly review and refine these rules to ensure they align with the organization's security policies and business requirements.

Overly permissive rules can expose the network to unnecessary risks, while overly restrictive rules can impede legitimate traffic and disrupt business operations.

Balancing security and functionality is crucial in this regard.

Additionally, organizations should implement stateful inspection, which tracks the state of active connections and allows only valid responses to outbound traffic.

This approach minimizes the attack surface and ensures that only traffic associated with established connections is permitted, enhancing both security and performance.

Firewall optimization also involves considering the principle of least privilege, where rules are configured to grant access only to the resources and services necessary for legitimate business operations.

Unnecessary access should be restricted to reduce the attack surface and limit potential security vulnerabilities.

To further optimize firewall performance, organizations should monitor firewall logs and alerts.

Regularly reviewing these logs can help identify unauthorized access attempts, unusual traffic patterns, or signs of a potential breach.

Swift response to security incidents and adjustments to firewall rules based on log data are essential for maintaining optimal security and performance.

Furthermore, organizations can segment their networks into zones and apply firewall rules to control traffic flow between these zones.

Network segmentation enhances security by isolating different network segments and limiting the lateral movement of attackers in the event of a breach.

Fine-tuning these zone-based rules ensures that network segments are appropriately isolated and that security policies are enforced consistently.

Firewall optimization extends to application layer firewall inspection.

These firewalls inspect and filter traffic based on application-layer protocols and content, allowing organizations to enforce policies on how applications are used within the network.

Fine-tuning application layer firewall rules involves creating rules that align with the organization's application usage policies and regularly reviewing and updating them to accommodate changing business requirements.

In addition, firewall optimization may involve integrating intrusion detection and prevention systems (IDPS) with firewalls.

IDPS solutions work alongside firewalls to identify and block known attack patterns and signatures.

Optimizing rules that govern IDPS integration ensures that organizations stay current with emerging threats and that their security controls are effective in detecting and preventing attacks.

To further enhance firewall performance, organizations can implement load balancing and failover mechanisms.

Load balancing distributes network traffic across multiple firewall devices, ensuring even distribution of traffic and preventing overloading of a single firewall.

Failover mechanisms provide redundancy, allowing traffic to be rerouted to a secondary firewall in case of a primary firewall failure, ensuring uninterrupted security protection.

Moreover, organizations can consider the use of application delivery controllers (ADCs) to optimize firewall performance.

ADCs help manage and optimize traffic flow to firewall devices, improving both security and network performance.

In summary, optimizing firewall performance is essential for maintaining robust network security while ensuring that business operations run smoothly.

It involves selecting the appropriate firewall type, ensuring hardware and software are up to date, fine-tuning rules and policies, implementing stateful inspection, and monitoring logs for security incidents.

Additionally, network segmentation, application layer firewall inspection, and integration with IDPS solutions are key elements of firewall optimization.

By considering these factors and striking the right balance between security and functionality, organizations can maximize the effectiveness of their firewalls and protect their digital assets from evolving threats.

In the realm of cybersecurity, optimizing firewall performance is a critical aspect of maintaining robust network security.

Firewalls are a fundamental component of any organization's security infrastructure, serving as the gatekeepers that control the flow of network traffic and protect against malicious threats.

However, for firewalls to effectively safeguard an organization's digital assets and data, their performance must be optimized to strike the right balance between security and functionality.

To achieve this balance, organizations must take several factors into consideration when optimizing their firewall performance.

One of the key factors in firewall optimization is selecting the appropriate type of firewall for the organization's specific needs.

There are different types of firewalls available, including stateful inspection firewalls, proxy firewalls, and application-layer firewalls, each with its own strengths and weaknesses.

Choosing the right type of firewall depends on factors such as the organization's network architecture, security requirements, and the types of threats it needs to defend against.

Once the appropriate firewall type is selected, organizations need to ensure that the firewall hardware and software are up to date and capable of handling the network traffic volume.

Outdated or insufficient hardware can lead to performance bottlenecks, resulting in slow network speeds and reduced security efficacy.

Regular hardware upgrades and software updates are essential to maintain optimal firewall performance.

Another critical aspect of firewall optimization is the fine-tuning of firewall rules and policies.

Firewalls rely on rules to determine which traffic is allowed or denied based on predefined criteria such as source and destination IP addresses, port numbers, and protocols.

To optimize firewall performance, organizations must regularly review and refine these rules to ensure they align with the organization's security policies and business requirements. Overly permissive rules can expose the network to unnecessary risks, while overly restrictive rules can impede legitimate traffic and disrupt business operations. Balancing security and functionality is crucial in this regard.

Additionally, organizations should implement stateful inspection, which tracks the state of active connections and allows only valid responses to outbound traffic. This approach minimizes the attack surface and ensures that only traffic associated with established connections is permitted, enhancing both security and performance.

Firewall optimization also involves considering the principle of least privilege, where rules are configured to grant access only to the resources and services necessary for legitimate business operations. Unnecessary access should be restricted to reduce the attack surface and limit potential security vulnerabilities.

To further optimize firewall performance, organizations should monitor firewall logs and alerts. Regularly reviewing these logs can help identify unauthorized access attempts, unusual traffic patterns, or signs of a potential breach.

Swift response to security incidents and adjustments to firewall rules based on log data are essential for maintaining optimal security and performance.

Furthermore, organizations can segment their networks into zones and apply firewall rules to control traffic flow between these zones.

Network segmentation enhances security by isolating different network segments and limiting the lateral movement of attackers in the event of a breach.

Fine-tuning these zone-based rules ensures that network segments are appropriately isolated and that security policies are enforced consistently.

Firewall optimization extends to application layer firewall inspection.

These firewalls inspect and filter traffic based on application-layer protocols and content, allowing organizations to enforce policies on how applications are used within the network.

Fine-tuning application layer firewall rules involves creating rules that align with the organization's application usage policies and regularly reviewing and updating them to accommodate changing business requirements.

In addition, firewall optimization may involve integrating intrusion detection and prevention systems (IDPS) with firewalls.

IDPS solutions work alongside firewalls to identify and block known attack patterns and signatures.

Optimizing rules that govern IDPS integration ensures that organizations stay current with emerging threats and that their security controls are effective in detecting and preventing attacks.

To further enhance firewall performance, organizations can implement load balancing and failover mechanisms.

Load balancing distributes network traffic across multiple firewall devices, ensuring even distribution of traffic and preventing overloading of a single firewall.

Failover mechanisms provide redundancy, allowing traffic to be rerouted to a secondary firewall in case of a primary firewall failure, ensuring uninterrupted security protection.

Moreover, organizations can consider the use of application delivery controllers (ADCs) to optimize firewall performance. ADCs help manage and optimize traffic flow to firewall devices, improving both security and network performance.

In summary, optimizing firewall performance is essential for maintaining robust network security while ensuring that business operations run smoothly.

It involves selecting the appropriate firewall type, ensuring hardware and software are up to date, fine-tuning rules and policies, implementing stateful inspection, and monitoring logs for security incidents.

Additionally, network segmentation, application layer firewall inspection, and integration with IDPS solutions are key elements of firewall optimization.

By considering these factors and striking the right balance between security and functionality, organizations can maximize the effectiveness of their firewalls and protect their digital assets from evolving threats.

Chapter 5: Intrusion Detection and Response at Scale

In the ever-evolving landscape of cybersecurity, Intrusion Detection Systems (IDS) and Intrusion Prevention Systems (IPS) are pivotal components that organizations rely on to safeguard their networks and data.

Scalable IDS/IPS solutions are essential to accommodate the increasing volume and complexity of cyber threats while maintaining optimal network performance.

When deploying scalable IDS/IPS solutions, organizations must consider several key factors to ensure they effectively protect their networks.

One crucial aspect of scalability is the ability to handle a growing number of network devices, endpoints, and traffic without compromising detection accuracy or responsiveness.

Scalable IDS/IPS solutions should be capable of analyzing and processing high volumes of network traffic efficiently.

Additionally, organizations should evaluate the scalability of IDS/IPS solutions based on their network architecture and traffic patterns.

Different networks may have unique scalability requirements, such as accommodating high-speed data centers or distributed branch offices.

It's essential to choose a solution that can adapt to the specific needs of the organization.

Scalable IDS/IPS solutions often leverage load balancing techniques to distribute network traffic evenly across multiple sensors or appliances.

Load balancing helps prevent overloading a single IDS/IPS device, ensuring that all network traffic is adequately analyzed and protected.

Moreover, failover mechanisms can be implemented to provide redundancy and ensure uninterrupted protection in case of sensor or appliance failures.

Organizations should also consider the deployment architecture of their IDS/IPS solution.

Scalable deployments may involve deploying sensors strategically at key points within the network, such as at the perimeter, within data centers, or in critical network segments.

These sensors should be able to work together seamlessly, sharing threat intelligence and providing coordinated protection across the entire network.

A centralized management console or platform is essential for monitoring and configuring IDS/IPS sensors efficiently.

This console should offer scalability in terms of managing an increasing number of sensors and providing a unified view of the entire network's security posture.

Furthermore, organizations should invest in solutions that support distributed deployments.

This allows for the flexible placement of sensors in geographically dispersed locations, ensuring comprehensive threat detection and prevention across the organization's entire footprint.

Scalable IDS/IPS solutions should provide the flexibility to adjust detection and prevention policies based on the organization's evolving security needs.

Customizable policies enable organizations to adapt to changing threats and compliance requirements.

Fine-tuning detection and prevention rules can optimize the solution's accuracy and reduce false positives, allowing security teams to focus on genuine threats.

When deploying scalable IDS/IPS solutions, organizations must consider the integration of threat intelligence feeds.

These feeds provide real-time information on emerging threats and known attack patterns.

Integrating threat intelligence helps IDS/IPS systems stay current and enables them to detect and prevent the latest cyber threats effectively.

Moreover, organizations should assess the scalability of their threat intelligence integration, ensuring it can accommodate a growing number of feeds and sources.

Scalable IDS/IPS solutions often incorporate machine learning and advanced analytics to enhance their detection capabilities.

These technologies enable the system to analyze large datasets and identify anomalous behavior that may signify a security breach.

Machine learning models can adapt and improve over time, making them valuable for scalable and evolving security needs.

It's crucial for organizations to evaluate the performance impact of these advanced capabilities on their network and ensure that the IDS/IPS solution can handle the computational demands.

Scalable IDS/IPS solutions should also support customizable reporting and alerting capabilities.

As the volume of network traffic and security events increases, it becomes essential to prioritize and manage alerts effectively.

Customizable reporting allows organizations to tailor alerts to their specific needs and focus on critical security incidents.

Scalable solutions should facilitate integration with Security Information and Event Management (SIEM) systems or security orchestration platforms.

These integrations enable organizations to centralize and correlate security event data from multiple sources, enhancing their overall security posture.

Furthermore, organizations should consider the scalability of their IDS/IPS solutions regarding the diversity of traffic they can analyze.

With the proliferation of encrypted traffic (SSL/TLS), scalable IDS/IPS solutions should include robust SSL/TLS decryption capabilities.

This enables the inspection of encrypted traffic for potential threats while maintaining privacy and compliance.

Additionally, organizations should ensure that their IDS/IPS solutions can adapt to new network protocols and application-layer traffic, as cyber threats constantly evolve.

Scalable IDS/IPS deployments often involve the use of virtual sensors or appliances.

Virtualization provides flexibility and scalability, allowing organizations to deploy sensors quickly and adjust their resources based on demand.

However, organizations should carefully manage and monitor resource allocation to ensure the continued effectiveness of virtual IDS/IPS sensors.

To maintain scalability, organizations should regularly assess the performance and capacity of their IDS/IPS solutions.

Load testing and performance tuning can help identify bottlenecks and ensure that the solution can handle increasing traffic volumes without compromising security.

Furthermore, organizations should consider scalability in terms of their IDS/IPS vendor partnerships.

Choosing a reputable vendor that offers a range of scalable solutions and provides ongoing support is essential for long-term success.

In summary, scalable IDS/IPS solutions are crucial in the face of evolving cyber threats and the ever-increasing volume of network traffic.

Organizations must carefully evaluate their scalability requirements, consider deployment architectures, integrate threat intelligence, leverage advanced technologies, and ensure the flexibility to adjust detection policies.

By prioritizing scalability, organizations can effectively protect their networks and data while adapting to the dynamic cybersecurity landscape.

In the realm of cybersecurity, advanced threat detection and rapid response have become paramount in defending against the relentless and sophisticated adversaries that target organizations and their digital assets. With the proliferation of increasingly complex threats, traditional security measures have proven inadequate in keeping up with the evolving tactics, techniques, and procedures employed by malicious actors.

As organizations embrace digital transformation and expand their attack surface through cloud adoption, IoT, and remote work, the need for advanced threat detection solutions has never been more urgent.

Advanced threat detection goes beyond traditional signature-based methods, which rely on known patterns of malicious activity, to incorporate behavioral analysis, machine learning, and artificial intelligence.

These cutting-edge technologies enable security systems to identify abnormal or suspicious behavior, even when dealing with previously unseen threats.

Behavioral analysis involves monitoring and profiling network and user activity to establish baselines of normal behavior.

By recognizing deviations from these baselines, security systems can raise alerts and investigate potential security incidents.

Machine learning algorithms play a vital role in advanced threat detection by continuously analyzing vast datasets to identify patterns and anomalies that may signify a cyber threat.

These algorithms adapt and improve their detection capabilities over time, making them invaluable in the ever-changing threat landscape.

Artificial intelligence further enhances threat detection by enabling systems to make autonomous decisions based on the analysis of large datasets and the identification of complex threat indicators.

The integration of these technologies into advanced threat detection solutions empowers organizations to identify threats faster and with greater accuracy.

One of the key advantages of advanced threat detection is its ability to detect zero-day vulnerabilities and attacks, which are previously unknown and lack established signatures.

Traditional security measures often struggle to protect against these threats, as they do not have predefined patterns to recognize.

Advanced threat detection systems excel in identifying and mitigating these attacks by focusing on unusual behavior or suspicious actions within the network.

Intrusion Detection Systems (IDS) and Intrusion Prevention Systems (IPS) are critical components of advanced threat detection.

These systems continuously monitor network traffic and analyze it for signs of malicious activity.

When suspicious activity is detected, IDS can issue alerts, while IPS can take automated actions to block or mitigate the threat.

To enhance rapid response, organizations should integrate their advanced threat detection solutions with Security Information and Event Management (SIEM) platforms.

SIEM systems collect and correlate data from various sources, including IDS/IPS, firewalls, and other security tools.

This centralized view of security events enables security teams to quickly identify and respond to threats.

Additionally, Threat Intelligence Feeds can provide valuable context and information about emerging threats and known attack techniques.

By integrating threat intelligence into their advanced threat detection systems, organizations can proactively defend against known threats and vulnerabilities.

Continuous monitoring is essential for effective advanced threat detection.

By continuously monitoring network traffic, user activity, and system logs, organizations can quickly identify anomalies and potential security incidents.

Regularly reviewing logs and conducting security audits can uncover vulnerabilities and misconfigurations that may be exploited by attackers.

User and entity behavior analytics (UEBA) is a crucial aspect of advanced threat detection.

UEBA solutions analyze user behavior and establish behavioral baselines for individual users and entities.

By monitoring deviations from these baselines, organizations can detect insider threats and unauthorized access promptly. Furthermore, UEBA can assist in identifying compromised accounts or devices.

Endpoint detection and response (EDR) solutions play a critical role in advanced threat detection at the endpoint level.

These solutions monitor and analyze activities on individual devices, providing valuable insights into potential threats and suspicious behavior.

When an EDR system detects a threat, it can initiate automated responses to isolate or remediate the affected endpoint.

Advanced threat detection also extends to the detection of advanced persistent threats (APTs).

APTs are sophisticated and often stealthy attacks that aim to infiltrate an organization's network over an extended period.

Advanced threat detection solutions are designed to detect and respond to APTs by identifying subtle indicators of compromise and unusual activity.

Incorporating threat hunting into the security strategy is another essential element of advanced threat detection.

Threat hunting involves proactively searching for signs of malicious activity within the network, even if no alerts have been triggered.

This proactive approach helps organizations identify and mitigate threats before they cause significant damage.

Automation and orchestration play a crucial role in rapidly responding to advanced threats.

By automating the response to certain types of threats, organizations can reduce the time it takes to mitigate the impact of an attack.

Orchestration platforms can streamline the coordination of various security tools and workflows, enabling a more efficient response to complex threats.

Collaboration and information sharing within the cybersecurity community are essential for advanced threat detection.

Information sharing allows organizations to learn from the experiences of others and stay informed about emerging threats and vulnerabilities.

Collaboration among security professionals can help identify patterns and trends in cyberattacks.

Organizations should also consider employing threat hunting teams and establishing a Security Operations Center (SOC) equipped with skilled analysts who specialize in advanced threat detection.

These teams play a critical role in investigating alerts, identifying false positives, and responding to confirmed security incidents.

Effective incident response plans are essential for rapidly addressing and mitigating advanced threats.

These plans should outline roles, responsibilities, and communication procedures to ensure a coordinated and efficient response to security incidents.

Regularly testing and refining incident response plans through tabletop exercises and simulations can help organizations improve their ability to respond effectively.

In summary, advanced threat detection and rapid response are indispensable components of a modern cybersecurity strategy.

As cyber threats continue to evolve and grow in sophistication, organizations must invest in advanced threat detection solutions that leverage behavioral analysis, machine learning, and artificial intelligence.

Integration with SIEM, threat intelligence feeds, and automation can further enhance the effectiveness of these solutions.

Continuous monitoring, user and entity behavior analytics, and endpoint detection and response are vital elements in identifying and responding to threats.

Threat hunting, automation, orchestration, collaboration, and incident response planning complete the toolkit for defending against advanced threats in today's digital landscape.

Chapter 6: Encryption, Key Management, and Secure Data Storage

In the ever-evolving landscape of cybersecurity, encryption remains one of the most fundamental and critical tools for safeguarding sensitive information and data privacy.

Advanced encryption algorithms play a pivotal role in securing data at rest, in transit, and during processing, providing a robust defense against unauthorized access and potential data breaches.

Encryption, at its core, is the process of converting plaintext information into ciphertext using a mathematical algorithm and a cryptographic key.

This transformation ensures that even if an attacker gains access to the encrypted data, it appears as gibberish without the proper decryption key.

The importance of encryption cannot be overstated, as it protects confidential data such as financial transactions, personal communications, and sensitive corporate information from prying eyes.

Over the years, encryption algorithms have evolved in response to advances in computing power and cryptographic research.

One of the most widely used encryption algorithms is the Advanced Encryption Standard (AES), which was established as the standard for encrypting data by the U.S. National Institute of Standards and Technology (NIST) in 2001.

AES operates on blocks of data, encrypting and decrypting them using symmetric keys, meaning the same key is used for both encryption and decryption.

Its strengths lie in its efficiency, speed, and resistance to known cryptographic attacks.

AES offers varying key lengths, with AES-128, AES-192, and AES-256, each providing a higher level of security.

Another well-known encryption algorithm is RSA (Rivest-Shamir-Adleman), which is an asymmetric algorithm that uses a pair of keys: a public key for encryption and a private key for decryption.

RSA is widely used for secure communication, digital signatures, and key exchange protocols.

The security of RSA is based on the difficulty of factoring the product of two large prime numbers, which serves as the foundation for its key pair.

ECC (Elliptic Curve Cryptography) is an asymmetric encryption algorithm gaining popularity due to its efficiency and strong security.

ECC relies on the mathematical properties of elliptic curves, making it suitable for resource-constrained environments such as mobile devices and IoT devices.

The efficiency of ECC allows for shorter key lengths while maintaining the same level of security as longer keys in other encryption algorithms.

One of the critical aspects of encryption is the management of cryptographic keys, which are the secret values used to encrypt and decrypt data.

The security of an encryption system hinges on the protection and proper handling of these keys.

Key management encompasses key generation, distribution, storage, rotation, and disposal.

Ensuring that keys are generated securely and kept confidential is paramount to the overall security of encrypted data.

Key distribution involves securely delivering keys to authorized parties without exposing them to interception or theft.

Key storage is another crucial aspect, as keys must be stored in a secure manner, away from potential threats.

Key rotation is the practice of periodically changing encryption keys to mitigate the risk of compromise.

Finally, key disposal involves securely erasing or rendering keys unreadable when they are no longer needed.

Implementing encryption correctly requires careful consideration of the encryption mode and padding scheme.

The mode of operation determines how the encryption algorithm is applied to plaintext data.

Common modes include Electronic Codebook (ECB), Cipher Block Chaining (CBC), and Galois/Counter Mode (GCM).

Each mode has its advantages and is suited to different use cases, depending on the required security guarantees.

Padding schemes are used to ensure that plaintext data is of a fixed block size, as most encryption algorithms operate on fixed-size blocks.

Inadequate padding schemes can introduce vulnerabilities, so choosing an appropriate one is crucial.

Ensuring that encryption keys are generated with sufficient entropy, or randomness, is essential to preventing predictable keys that can be easily guessed or brute-forced.

Random number generators (RNGs) are employed to generate cryptographic keys securely.

Secure key storage solutions, such as Hardware Security Modules (HSMs), provide a high level of protection for encryption keys by keeping them isolated from the host system and potential attackers.

HSMs offer physical and logical security controls, making them a trusted choice for safeguarding keys in critical environments.

End-to-end encryption is a practice that ensures data remains encrypted throughout its entire journey, from the sender to the recipient, without any intermediate parties having access to the unencrypted data.

This approach is commonly used in secure messaging apps, email services, and online banking to protect sensitive information from eavesdropping or interception.

Quantum computing represents a potential threat to current encryption algorithms.

Quantum computers have the potential to break widely used encryption methods, including RSA and ECC, through their ability to perform certain mathematical calculations much faster than classical computers. To prepare for this potential threat, researchers are actively developing quantum-resistant encryption algorithms that can withstand attacks from quantum computers. Post-quantum cryptography is an emerging field focused on designing encryption methods that are resilient to quantum attacks.

It is essential for organizations to keep abreast of developments in post-quantum cryptography and prepare for a transition to quantum-resistant encryption when necessary. In summary, advanced encryption algorithms are the cornerstone of data security in the digital age.

These algorithms, such as AES, RSA, and ECC, provide the means to protect sensitive information and communications from unauthorized access.

Effective encryption relies not only on the choice of a robust algorithm but also on sound key management practices, secure implementation, and careful consideration of encryption modes and padding schemes.

As quantum computing advances, the field of post-quantum cryptography will become increasingly important to maintain the security of encrypted data in the face of evolving threats.

Key management and secure storage are critical aspects of maintaining the confidentiality and integrity of sensitive information in any organization.

In today's digital landscape, where data breaches and cyberattacks are on the rise, a robust key management strategy is essential to protect cryptographic keys from unauthorized access and potential compromise.

One of the fundamental principles of key management is to generate keys with sufficient entropy, or randomness.

High entropy keys are less predictable, making them more resistant to brute-force attacks or other methods of key discovery.

Random number generators (RNGs) are commonly used to generate cryptographic keys securely, ensuring that they are truly random and not susceptible to predictability.

Once cryptographic keys are generated, they must be securely stored to prevent unauthorized access.

The importance of secure key storage cannot be overstated, as the compromise of a cryptographic key can lead to the exposure of sensitive data.

Hardware Security Modules (HSMs) are specialized devices designed to securely store and manage cryptographic keys.

HSMs provide both physical and logical protection for keys, making them a trusted choice for key storage in critical environments.

Physical security measures, such as tamper-evident seals and strong enclosures, protect HSMs from physical attacks, while access control policies restrict who can access the keys and under what circumstances.

Another key storage consideration is redundancy and backup.

Organizations should implement backup procedures to ensure that keys are not lost due to hardware failures or other unforeseen events.

Regularly scheduled key rotation is a recommended practice to limit the exposure of a key.

By periodically generating new keys and retiring old ones, organizations can mitigate the risk associated with long-term key compromise.

Key rotation is particularly important when dealing with keys used for encryption, digital signatures, or access control.

It's essential to keep detailed records of key usage and rotation to maintain accountability and traceability.

Access to cryptographic keys should be restricted to authorized personnel who have a legitimate need to use them.

Access control policies should be enforced to ensure that only approved individuals can manage and retrieve keys.

Multi-factor authentication (MFA) can enhance security by requiring multiple forms of verification before granting access to key management systems.

Role-based access control (RBAC) is another effective approach to controlling who can perform specific actions with cryptographic keys.

When it comes to cryptographic key distribution, secure channels and protocols must be used to prevent key interception or tampering.

Secure Sockets Layer (SSL) and Transport Layer Security (TLS) are commonly employed to protect key exchange during secure communications.

In cases where keys need to be shared between different entities, secure key exchange protocols like Diffie-Hellman key exchange can be utilized.

Organizations should regularly review and update their key management policies and practices to ensure they remain effective in the face of evolving threats and compliance requirements.

Periodic security audits and assessments can help identify vulnerabilities and areas for improvement in the key management process.

It's crucial to maintain an accurate inventory of all cryptographic keys in use, including their purposes and associated metadata.

This inventory helps ensure that no keys are forgotten or overlooked during key rotation or retirement.

Additionally, organizations should establish incident response procedures specifically tailored to key compromise scenarios.

In the event that a key is suspected to be compromised or exposed, swift action must be taken to mitigate the potential impact on data security.

This may involve key rotation, revocation, or other remediation measures.

Key escrow, a process in which a third party holds a copy of cryptographic keys, can provide a recovery mechanism in case of key loss or compromise.

However, key escrow should be implemented cautiously, as it introduces its own security and privacy considerations.

In summary, key management and secure key storage are integral components of a comprehensive cybersecurity strategy.

Effective key management practices, such as high-entropy key generation, secure storage with HSMs, access control policies, key rotation, and regular audits, are essential to safeguarding cryptographic keys and, by extension, the sensitive data they protect.

By adhering to best practices in key management, organizations can significantly enhance their data security posture and mitigate the risk of key-related security breaches.

Chapter 7: Identity and Access Management Beyond Basics

Identity and Access Management (IAM) plays a critical role in modern cybersecurity by ensuring that only authorized individuals or entities have access to an organization's resources and data. As organizations grow and adopt diverse technologies, the need for advanced IAM solutions becomes increasingly apparent. Advanced IAM solutions go beyond traditional username and password authentication, offering multifaceted approaches to identity verification and access control. These solutions are designed to enhance security, streamline user management, and facilitate access to resources while reducing the risks associated with unauthorized access.

One key element of advanced IAM solutions is the implementation of Multi-Factor Authentication (MFA). MFA adds an extra layer of security by requiring users to provide multiple forms of identification before gaining access to a system or application. This often includes something the user knows (e.g., a password), something the user has (e.g., a smartphone with a one-time code generator), and something the user is (e.g., a fingerprint or facial recognition). MFA significantly reduces the likelihood of unauthorized access, even if a password is compromised.

Identity Federation is another critical aspect of advanced IAM solutions. Federation allows users to access multiple applications and systems using a single set of credentials. This streamlines the login process for users and simplifies identity management for administrators. Federation standards like Security Assertion Markup Language (SAML) and OpenID Connect enable secure identity propagation across different domains and services, promoting seamless user experiences without compromising security.

Privileged Access Management (PAM) is a crucial component of advanced IAM solutions, especially in organizations with complex IT environments. PAM focuses on controlling and monitoring privileged accounts, such as those used by administrators, to prevent abuse or unauthorized access. It encompasses features like just-in-time access, session recording, and privileged account discovery. By limiting access to privileged accounts to only when necessary and closely monitoring activities, PAM helps organizations safeguard critical systems and data.

Advanced IAM solutions also incorporate Adaptive Authentication, which evaluates user behavior and context to determine the level of access granted. Instead of applying a one-size-fits-all approach, adaptive authentication adjusts security measures based on the perceived risk. For example, if a user typically accesses a system from a corporate office during business hours but suddenly attempts to log in from an unfamiliar location at night, the system may prompt for additional authentication steps to confirm the user's identity.

Role-Based Access Control (RBAC) is an essential feature in advanced IAM solutions. RBAC assigns permissions to users based on their roles within the organization. By defining roles and associating them with specific access rights, organizations can efficiently manage access privileges across different departments and teams. This approach reduces the risk of granting excessive permissions and simplifies the process of revoking access when needed.

Advanced IAM solutions often integrate with Single Sign-On (SSO) capabilities, enabling users to access multiple applications with a single set of credentials. SSO enhances user convenience while maintaining strong security. Users don't have to remember multiple passwords for various services, reducing the likelihood of password-related security incidents like password reuse.

Access Governance and Compliance Management are crucial aspects of advanced IAM solutions. These features help organizations ensure that access policies align with regulatory requirements and internal security policies. Access governance provides visibility into who has access to what resources, allowing organizations to identify and remediate access discrepancies or violations proactively.

User Behavior Analytics (UBA) is another advanced IAM capability that focuses on detecting abnormal or suspicious user behavior patterns. UBA solutions use machine learning and behavioral analysis to identify deviations from typical user activities. By detecting anomalies early, organizations can respond to potential security threats before they escalate.

Advanced IAM solutions also facilitate the management of external identities, such as customers, partners, and vendors, through Identity as a Service (IDaaS) offerings. IDaaS platforms enable organizations to extend their IAM capabilities beyond internal users and provide secure access to external stakeholders while maintaining control and visibility.

Identity Lifecycle Management (ILM) is a critical component of advanced IAM, ensuring that user access is provisioned and deprovisioned efficiently throughout their lifecycle within an organization. Automated ILM processes help organizations reduce the risk of orphaned accounts and ensure that access is revoked promptly when a user leaves the organization.

In summary, advanced IAM solutions are essential for organizations looking to enhance their cybersecurity posture in an increasingly complex digital landscape. These solutions incorporate multifactor authentication, identity federation, privileged access management, adaptive authentication, role-based access control, single sign-on, access governance, user behavior analytics, and other features to provide robust identity and access management capabilities. By adopting advanced IAM solutions, organizations can strike a balance between security and user convenience, reduce the risk of unauthorized access, and meet compliance requirements effectively.

Privileged Access Management (PAM) and Role-Based Control (RBAC) are two crucial components of modern cybersecurity strategies. PAM focuses on managing and monitoring privileged accounts and access, while RBAC defines access rights based on individuals' roles within an organization. These two concepts work in tandem to ensure that only authorized users have access to critical systems, data, and resources.

PAM is essential because privileged accounts, often held by administrators and superusers, have elevated access privileges that can pose significant security risks if misused or compromised. PAM solutions are designed to control, monitor, and audit privileged access to mitigate these risks. One fundamental aspect of PAM is the principle of least privilege, which restricts users to only the permissions necessary for their specific tasks, reducing the potential for abuse or accidental damage.

Effective PAM solutions incorporate several key features. Just-in-Time (JIT) access is one such feature that allows users to request temporary elevated privileges only when needed, reducing the exposure of privileged accounts. Session recording and monitoring provide detailed logs of privileged access activities, enabling organizations to review and audit actions for compliance and security purposes.

Privileged Account Discovery is another important aspect of PAM, as it helps organizations identify and manage all privileged accounts across their IT landscape. Often, organizations may not have a complete inventory of these accounts, making it challenging to secure them adequately. PAM solutions aid in the identification and centralized management of privileged accounts, ensuring that they receive appropriate protection.

Role-Based Control, on the other hand, focuses on structuring access rights based on the roles and responsibilities of individuals within an organization. RBAC simplifies the management of user permissions by grouping users with similar job functions and defining access privileges accordingly. This approach streamlines access management, reducing the complexity of assigning and revoking permissions for individual users.

RBAC is particularly effective in large organizations with diverse teams and departments. By assigning roles and associating them with predefined access rights, administrators can maintain consistency in access control while adhering to the principle of least privilege. This reduces the likelihood of over-privileged accounts or permissions that could lead to security vulnerabilities.

In RBAC implementations, roles are typically defined based on job titles or functions within an organization. For example, a financial analyst role may grant access to financial systems and data, while a system administrator role may have broader access to manage IT infrastructure. Users are then assigned to these roles based on their job responsibilities, and their access permissions are automatically adjusted accordingly.

The integration of PAM and RBAC is a powerful strategy for securing an organization's digital assets. PAM solutions ensure that privileged access, which can have a more significant impact if misused, is tightly controlled and monitored. RBAC complements this by extending the same disciplined access control approach to all users, ensuring that access rights are appropriate and well-defined based on their roles.

To implement an effective PAM and RBAC strategy, organizations should first conduct a thorough assessment of their privileged accounts and access requirements. This involves identifying all privileged accounts, understanding the scope of their access, and categorizing them based on the level of privilege they possess.

Once privileged accounts are cataloged, organizations can establish RBAC policies by defining roles and their associated access rights. These policies should align with the organization's security and compliance requirements and be periodically reviewed and updated to adapt to changing needs.

PAM solutions can then be deployed to enforce RBAC policies by providing granular control over privileged access. JIT access, session recording, and monitoring capabilities should be configured to align with RBAC policies, ensuring that privileged access aligns with user roles and responsibilities.

Additionally, organizations should regularly audit and review both PAM and RBAC configurations to identify any discrepancies or security risks. Periodic assessments and compliance checks help ensure that the combined PAM and RBAC strategy remains effective in mitigating security threats and meeting regulatory requirements.

In summary, Privileged Access Management (PAM) and Role-Based Control (RBAC) are essential components of a comprehensive cybersecurity strategy. PAM focuses on securing and monitoring privileged access, while RBAC defines access rights based on user roles. Together, these two approaches provide a layered security framework that reduces the risk of unauthorized access and ensures that access permissions align with users' responsibilities within the organization. Implementing PAM and RBAC requires a systematic approach, including cataloging privileged accounts, defining roles and access rights, deploying PAM solutions, and regularly auditing and reviewing configurations to maintain security and compliance.

Chapter 8: Advanced Security Analytics and SIEM Integration

In the rapidly evolving landscape of cybersecurity, the volume, variety, and velocity of data generated by digital systems have grown exponentially, giving rise to the concept of Big Data. Leveraging Big Data for advanced security analytics has become essential for organizations seeking to detect and respond to emerging threats effectively. This chapter explores the significance of Big Data in the realm of cybersecurity and how it can be harnessed to enhance an organization's security posture.

At the heart of Big Data security analytics is the idea that large datasets can provide valuable insights into potential security breaches, anomalies, and patterns that might go unnoticed in smaller, traditional datasets. The sheer scale of data generated by modern networks and systems makes it impossible to manually process and analyze, necessitating automated and intelligent approaches to data analysis.

One of the primary benefits of using Big Data for security analytics is the ability to detect sophisticated and previously unknown threats. Traditional security tools often rely on predefined signatures or patterns, making them less effective at identifying novel attack methods or zero-day vulnerabilities. Big Data analytics, on the other hand, can analyze vast amounts of data in real-time and apply machine learning and behavioral analysis techniques to identify abnormal activities that could indicate a breach.

The data sources for Big Data security analytics are diverse and encompass network logs, system logs, application logs, user behavior data, threat intelligence feeds, and more. These sources collectively create a rich and multifaceted dataset that can be used to build a comprehensive understanding of an organization's security posture.

To effectively utilize Big Data for security analytics, organizations must invest in robust data collection and storage infrastructure. This includes the implementation of data lakes or warehouses capable of ingesting and storing massive volumes of data. Additionally, organizations must deploy advanced data analytics tools and platforms that can process and analyze the data efficiently.

Machine learning plays a critical role in Big Data security analytics by enabling predictive and prescriptive analysis. Machine learning models can be trained on historical data to identify normal patterns and behaviors within an organization's network. When deviations from these patterns occur, the models can trigger alerts or automated responses, helping security teams detect and respond to potential threats swiftly.

One of the key advantages of machine learning in security analytics is its ability to adapt to evolving threats. As cybercriminals continuously develop new attack techniques, machine learning models can learn and evolve to detect these novel threats. This adaptability is crucial in an environment where the threat landscape is constantly changing.

Real-time analysis is another critical aspect of Big Data security analytics. In a world where cyberattacks can happen at any moment, organizations need the ability to detect and respond to threats as they occur. Big Data analytics platforms can process data in real-time or near-real-time, enabling organizations to identify and mitigate threats as they unfold.

Visualization tools are instrumental in making sense of the insights generated by Big Data security analytics. Visual representations of data can help security analysts quickly grasp complex patterns and anomalies. Dashboards and reports can provide a consolidated view of an organization's security posture, making it easier to prioritize and respond to incidents.

One of the challenges of Big Data security analytics is the need for skilled data scientists and analysts who can interpret the results and make informed decisions. Organizations must invest in training and talent acquisition to build a team capable of effectively leveraging Big Data for security.

Another consideration is data privacy and compliance. When collecting and analyzing large volumes of data, organizations must ensure that they are adhering to relevant privacy regulations and industry standards. This includes anonymizing sensitive information and implementing strong access controls to protect data integrity.

In summary, the utilization of Big Data for advanced security analytics is a critical component of modern cybersecurity strategies. The vast amount of data generated by digital systems offers valuable insights into potential security threats and vulnerabilities. By harnessing Big Data analytics, organizations can detect and respond to emerging threats, adapt to evolving attack techniques, and improve their overall security posture. However, achieving effective Big Data security analytics requires the right infrastructure, machine learning capabilities, real-time analysis, visualization tools, and a skilled workforce. Moreover, organizations must also prioritize data privacy and compliance to ensure they are handling data responsibly and ethically.

In today's dynamic and ever-evolving cybersecurity landscape, organizations face a constant barrage of sophisticated and increasingly stealthy threats. To effectively defend against these threats, security professionals need not only the right tools and strategies but also access to timely and relevant threat intelligence. Security Information and Event Management (SIEM) systems have become central to an organization's ability to monitor, detect, and respond to security incidents. This chapter delves into the crucial integration of SIEM with threat intelligence to enhance an organization's threat detection capabilities.

SIEM systems are designed to collect and aggregate data from various sources within an organization's IT infrastructure. These sources include network devices, servers, firewalls, intrusion detection systems, and more. SIEM tools provide a centralized platform for analyzing this data, identifying security events, and generating alerts when suspicious activities are detected.

However, SIEM systems rely on predefined rules and patterns to detect anomalies and potential security incidents. While this approach is effective to a certain extent, it may miss emerging threats and zero-day vulnerabilities. This is where threat intelligence comes into play.

Threat intelligence is a valuable resource that provides organizations with insights into the current threat landscape. It encompasses information about known malicious actors, their tactics, techniques, and procedures (TTPs), indicators of compromise (IOCs), and other relevant data. Threat intelligence can be categorized into several types, including open-source threat intelligence, commercial threat feeds, and internally generated threat data.

Integrating threat intelligence with a SIEM system involves feeding this intelligence into the SIEM's analytical engine. This enables the SIEM to correlate security events and log data with threat intelligence feeds in real-time. The integration process can be accomplished through various methods, such as API integrations, direct data feeds, or manual data imports, depending on the SIEM's capabilities and the threat intelligence source.

The benefits of integrating SIEM with threat intelligence are numerous. Firstly, it enhances the SIEM's ability to detect and prioritize security events accurately. By cross-referencing incoming data with threat intelligence feeds, the SIEM can identify known attack patterns and IOCs, allowing security teams to respond swiftly to threats.

Secondly, threat intelligence enriches security alerts with contextual information. Instead of receiving generic alerts, analysts can gain insights into the specific threat actor behind an incident, their motivations, and the potential impact on the organization. This contextual information is invaluable for making informed decisions and responding effectively.

Thirdly, integrating threat intelligence enables proactive threat hunting. Security teams can use threat intelligence data to search for hidden threats and vulnerabilities within their network. By identifying patterns that align with known TTPs, they can uncover previously undetected threats and take steps to mitigate them.

Furthermore, SIEM and threat intelligence integration aids in the detection of advanced persistent threats (APTs). APTs are often highly targeted and sophisticated, designed to evade traditional security measures. With access to up-to-date threat intelligence, organizations can better recognize the indicators of an APT campaign and respond before significant damage occurs.

It's important to note that threat intelligence is not a one-size-fits-all solution. Organizations must carefully select and tailor threat intelligence sources to their specific industry, risk profile, and network environment. This ensures that the threat intelligence received is relevant and actionable.

Automation plays a vital role in maximizing the benefits of SIEM and threat intelligence integration. Many SIEM systems support automated responses to security incidents. When a SIEM detects a security event correlated with threat intelligence, it can trigger predefined actions, such as isolating compromised systems, blocking malicious IP addresses, or generating incident reports. This automation helps organizations respond rapidly to threats, reducing the time-to-mitigation.

The integration of SIEM with threat intelligence is not a one-time effort. It requires ongoing maintenance and updates to ensure that the threat intelligence feeds remain accurate and relevant. Threat actors are continually evolving their tactics, and threat intelligence must keep pace.

Moreover, organizations must establish a clear incident response plan that outlines how they will react to security incidents detected through SIEM and threat intelligence integration. This plan should define roles and responsibilities, escalation procedures, and communication protocols to ensure a coordinated and effective response.

In summary, the integration of SIEM with threat intelligence is a crucial strategy for enhancing an organization's ability to detect and respond to security threats. By leveraging up-to-date threat intelligence data, SIEM systems can identify known attack patterns, prioritize alerts, and provide context for security incidents. This integration is particularly valuable in the face of advanced and persistent threats, helping organizations stay one step ahead of cyber adversaries. However, organizations must carefully select and maintain their threat intelligence sources and establish clear incident response procedures to maximize the effectiveness of this integration.

Chapter 9: Incident Response Orchestration and Automation

In today's rapidly evolving cybersecurity landscape, organizations face a constant barrage of threats, ranging from malware infections to sophisticated cyberattacks. As the volume and complexity of these threats continue to increase, the need for efficient incident response processes becomes paramount. To address this challenge, organizations are turning to automation to streamline their incident response workflows.

Automating incident response workflows involves leveraging technology and predefined processes to detect, analyze, and mitigate security incidents in a more efficient and timely manner. This approach not only reduces response times but also minimizes the risk of human error, ultimately enhancing an organization's overall cybersecurity posture.

One of the primary benefits of automating incident response is the ability to detect and respond to threats in real-time or near-real-time. Traditional incident response methods often rely on manual analysis and decision-making, which can introduce delays that are unacceptable in today's threat landscape. With automation, security tools can analyze incoming data, identify potential security incidents, and trigger predefined response actions without human intervention.

For example, when a security information and event management (SIEM) system detects an unauthorized login attempt, it can automatically block the source IP address, preventing further intrusion attempts. This rapid response can thwart attacks before they escalate, reducing the potential impact on the organization.

Automation also plays a crucial role in ensuring consistent and standardized incident response procedures. By defining workflows and response actions in advance, organizations can ensure that every incident is handled according to best practices and compliance requirements. This consistency is especially important for organizations subject to regulatory frameworks that mandate specific incident response processes.

Furthermore, automation can help organizations prioritize incidents based on their severity and potential impact. Security tools can assign risk scores to incidents and prioritize the most critical ones for immediate attention. This enables security teams to focus their efforts on addressing the most pressing threats, rather than getting overwhelmed by a high volume of alerts.

Automated incident response also extends to the documentation and reporting aspects of security incidents. When an incident is resolved, automation can generate detailed reports, including the incident's timeline, actions taken, and lessons learned. These reports are invaluable for post-incident analysis and can help organizations fine-tune their incident response procedures for the future.

To implement automated incident response workflows effectively, organizations should follow a few key steps. First and foremost, they must identify the specific security incidents that can benefit from automation. Not all incidents require the same level of automation, and organizations should prioritize those that pose the greatest risk.

Next, organizations should invest in the right tools and technologies to support automation. This may include SIEM systems, security orchestration and automation platforms (SOAR), and threat intelligence feeds. These tools should be integrated seamlessly into the organization's existing security infrastructure to ensure a cohesive and efficient incident response ecosystem.

Once the tools are in place, organizations must define and document their incident response workflows. This includes specifying the conditions under which automation should trigger, the response actions to be taken, and the criteria for escalating incidents to human analysts. Clear documentation is essential to ensure that all stakeholders understand the automated processes and their roles in incident response.

Regular testing and validation of automated incident response workflows are also crucial. Organizations should conduct tabletop exercises and simulations to verify that the automation processes function as intended. This helps identify any gaps or issues in the workflow and allows for adjustments and improvements.

Additionally, organizations should continually update and refine their automation processes to adapt to evolving threats and technologies. Threat actors are constantly changing their tactics, and incident response workflows must be agile and responsive to these changes.

Finally, it's essential to strike the right balance between automation and human intervention. While automation can significantly expedite incident response, there will always be situations that require human judgment and decision-making. Organizations should establish clear guidelines for when human analysts should step in and take control of an incident.

In summary, automating incident response workflows is a critical component of modern cybersecurity strategies. It allows organizations to detect, analyze, and mitigate security incidents with greater speed, consistency, and efficiency. By leveraging technology and predefined processes, organizations can stay ahead of cyber threats and minimize the potential impact of security incidents. However, successful automation requires careful planning, integration, documentation, and ongoing refinement to ensure that incident response processes remain effective in a constantly evolving threat landscape.

In the dynamic and complex world of cybersecurity, orchestrating multi-stage incident response is an essential strategy to effectively combat advanced threats and security breaches. Incidents in today's digital landscape rarely present themselves as isolated events; instead, they often unfold across multiple stages and vectors, requiring a coordinated and multifaceted response.

Multi-stage incident response is a comprehensive approach that recognizes the interconnected nature of security incidents and aims to contain, investigate, and mitigate them across various phases. This approach is particularly crucial for dealing with advanced persistent threats (APTs), which can operate stealthily and persistently within a network, evading detection for extended periods.

The first stage of multi-stage incident response is detection. Detecting security incidents is the foundation of an effective response. This involves the continuous monitoring of network and system activities for signs of abnormal behavior or potential breaches. Detection methods range from intrusion detection systems (IDS) and intrusion prevention systems (IPS) to advanced threat detection solutions powered by artificial intelligence and machine learning.

Upon detection, the incident response team initiates the second stage: containment. Containment aims to prevent the incident from spreading further within the network. This may involve isolating affected systems, blocking malicious communication channels, and closing vulnerabilities that the attackers exploited. Effective containment limits the scope of the incident, reducing potential damage.

With containment in place, the incident response team proceeds to the investigation phase. This stage is critical for understanding the nature and scope of the incident, as well as identifying the attackers' tactics, techniques, and objectives. Investigation methods include digital forensics, log analysis, and threat intelligence gathering. The goal is to gather evidence, assess the impact, and determine the root cause of the incident.

Once the incident has been thoroughly investigated, the response team enters the mitigation phase. Mitigation involves taking corrective actions to eliminate the vulnerabilities that allowed the incident to occur in the first place. This may include patching software, updating configurations, and enhancing security controls to prevent similar incidents in the future.

Simultaneously, during the investigation and mitigation stages, organizations often engage in the communication and coordination aspect of incident response. This involves liaising with relevant stakeholders, such as legal teams, law enforcement, and public relations, to manage the incident's impact and comply with regulatory requirements. Effective communication is essential for maintaining transparency and trust with customers, partners, and the public.

The fifth stage of multi-stage incident response focuses on eradication. Eradication goes beyond containment and aims to completely remove all traces of the attacker's presence from the network. This step often requires a thorough review of the network infrastructure, application code, and user accounts to ensure that no backdoors or persistent threats remain.

Following eradication, organizations move into the recovery phase. Recovery efforts are designed to restore normal business operations and minimize downtime. This may involve restoring data from backups, rebuilding compromised systems, and implementing additional security measures to prevent similar incidents.

The final stage of multi-stage incident response is lessons learned and documentation. After resolving the incident, organizations conduct a post-incident analysis to assess the effectiveness of their response and identify areas for improvement. Detailed documentation of the incident, including timelines, actions taken, and outcomes, is crucial for future incident prevention and response planning.

Implementing a successful multi-stage incident response strategy requires a combination of technology, processes, and skilled personnel. Security tools, such as SIEM systems, forensic software, and threat intelligence feeds, play a vital role in detection, investigation, and mitigation. Additionally, well-defined incident response plans, including roles and responsibilities, are essential for coordinating efforts during an incident.

Furthermore, organizations must invest in continuous training and skill development for their incident response teams. Staying up-to-date with evolving threats and emerging attack vectors is essential to maintaining an effective multi-stage incident response capability.

In summary, orchestrating multi-stage incident response is a holistic approach to cybersecurity that acknowledges the intricate nature of modern security incidents. By seamlessly transitioning through the stages of detection, containment, investigation, mitigation, communication, eradication, recovery, and lessons learned, organizations can effectively manage and mitigate the impact of security incidents. This approach not only enhances an organization's security posture but also helps build resilience and preparedness in the face of evolving cyber threats.

Chapter 10: Cyber Resilience Frameworks and Beyond

Cyber resilience maturity models are valuable tools that organizations can use to assess and enhance their ability to withstand and recover from cyber threats and incidents. These models provide a structured framework for evaluating an organization's cyber resilience posture and identifying areas for improvement.

At the core of cyber resilience maturity models is the recognition that cybersecurity is not just about preventing attacks but also about preparing for and responding to them effectively. Cyber resilience goes beyond traditional cybersecurity measures by emphasizing an organization's capacity to adapt and recover in the face of cyber disruptions.

One commonly used cyber resilience maturity model is the Cyber Resilience Maturity Model (CRMM), which was developed by the CERT Division of Carnegie Mellon University's Software Engineering Institute (SEI). The CRMM consists of five maturity levels, each representing a higher degree of cyber resilience.

The first level, known as "Initial," is characterized by an organization's limited ability to manage and respond to cyber incidents. Organizations at this stage often lack formalized incident response procedures and may have limited cybersecurity awareness among their staff.

Moving up to the "Managed" level, organizations begin to establish foundational cybersecurity practices. They develop incident response plans, conduct risk assessments, and implement basic security controls. However, their cyber resilience capabilities are still relatively reactive.

The "Defined" level marks a significant step forward in an organization's cyber resilience journey. At this stage, organizations have well-defined processes and procedures in place for incident response and recovery. They actively monitor their networks and systems, perform regular assessments, and continuously improve their cybersecurity posture.

Achieving the "Quantitatively Managed" level indicates that an organization has reached a high level of maturity in cyber resilience. At this stage, organizations not only have robust incident response capabilities but also measure and analyze the effectiveness of their cybersecurity measures. They use data and metrics to drive continuous improvement in their cyber resilience practices.

The highest level, "Optimizing," represents organizations that have fully integrated cyber resilience into their overall business strategy. These organizations proactively seek out vulnerabilities and weaknesses, implement advanced threat detection and prevention technologies, and have a strong culture of security awareness throughout the organization.

Implementing a cyber resilience maturity model involves several key steps. First, an organization must assess its current state by evaluating its existing cybersecurity practices, incident response capabilities, and overall resilience posture. This assessment should involve all relevant stakeholders, from IT and security teams to executive leadership.

Next, the organization should set clear goals for improving its cyber resilience maturity. These goals should be specific, measurable, achievable, relevant, and time-bound (SMART), and they should align with the organization's overall business objectives.

Once goals are established, the organization can create a roadmap for achieving them. This roadmap should outline the steps, resources, and timelines required to move from the current maturity level to the desired level.

One essential aspect of implementing a cyber resilience maturity model is the continuous monitoring and measurement of progress. Organizations should regularly assess their cyber resilience posture, track key performance indicators (KPIs), and adjust their strategies as needed to stay on course toward their goals.

Cyber resilience maturity models are not one-size-fits-all solutions. Organizations may choose to adapt existing models or develop custom models that better align with their specific needs and industry requirements. Regardless of the chosen model, the goal is to improve an organization's ability to detect, respond to, and recover from cyber incidents.

In addition to the CRMM, other industry-specific cyber resilience maturity models exist, such as the NIST Cybersecurity Framework and the ISO 27001 standard. These frameworks provide valuable guidelines and best practices for enhancing cyber resilience.

Overall, cyber resilience maturity models are essential tools for organizations seeking to navigate the ever-evolving landscape of cyber threats and incidents. By assessing their current state, setting clear goals, and following a structured approach to improvement, organizations can build a strong foundation for cyber resilience and better protect their critical assets and operations.

In the ever-evolving world of cybersecurity, the concept of cyber resilience has become increasingly vital. It transcends the traditional boundaries of cybersecurity frameworks and demands a more adaptive and dynamic approach to protect organizations from the relentless onslaught of cyber threats. While frameworks like NIST's Cybersecurity Framework and

ISO 27001 provide valuable guidelines, they may fall short in addressing the rapidly changing threat landscape.

Adaptive cyber resilience strategies recognize that the nature of cyber threats is inherently dynamic. Attack techniques evolve, threat actors become more sophisticated, and vulnerabilities are discovered and exploited faster than ever before. Therefore, organizations must go beyond static frameworks and adopt a mindset that embraces change and continuous improvement.

One fundamental aspect of adaptive cyber resilience is the acknowledgment that cybersecurity is not solely the responsibility of the IT department but a shared responsibility throughout the entire organization. Employees, from the C-suite to front-line staff, play a crucial role in defending against cyber threats. A culture of cybersecurity awareness and vigilance must permeate the organization's DNA.

An adaptive cyber resilience strategy starts with robust risk management. Organizations should continuously assess their risk landscape, taking into account emerging threats and vulnerabilities. Risk assessments should be agile and responsive, allowing for rapid adjustments as new information becomes available. Risk tolerance levels should be clearly defined and communicated throughout the organization.

Incident response is another critical component of adaptive cyber resilience. Traditional incident response plans may no longer suffice in a fast-paced threat environment. Organizations should develop agile incident response procedures that can adapt to evolving threats and prioritize rapid containment and recovery. Regular drills and exercises can help teams refine their response capabilities.

A key principle of adaptive cyber resilience is the assumption that breaches will occur. No defense is impenetrable, and organizations should prepare for the inevitability of incidents. This preparation involves not only technical measures but also legal and communication strategies. Understanding the legal and regulatory implications of a breach and having a well-defined communication plan can mitigate the fallout from a cybersecurity incident.

In the context of adaptive cyber resilience, threat intelligence takes on a more prominent role. Organizations should establish robust threat intelligence programs that provide real-time information on emerging threats and tactics. This intelligence should inform not only defensive measures but also proactive threat hunting activities.

Threat hunting is an essential element of an adaptive cyber resilience strategy. Rather than relying solely on automated tools to detect threats, organizations should empower skilled analysts to actively seek out signs of compromise within their networks. Threat hunters can uncover hidden threats that automated systems may miss.

As cloud computing and virtualization technologies become increasingly prevalent, organizations must extend their adaptive cyber resilience strategies to these environments. Cloud security requires a different approach, with a focus on identity and access management, data encryption, and continuous monitoring. Organizations should also consider the shared responsibility model, which delineates security responsibilities between cloud providers and customers.

The concept of "zero trust" aligns closely with adaptive cyber resilience. Zero trust assumes that threats may exist both outside and inside the network. As such, it requires continuous authentication and authorization of users and devices, regardless of their location within the network. Implementing a zero-trust architecture can significantly enhance an organization's cyber resilience.

Machine learning and artificial intelligence (AI) are increasingly integrated into adaptive cyber resilience strategies. These technologies can analyze vast amounts of data and identify anomalous behavior more quickly than human analysts. However, their effectiveness depends on high-quality data and ongoing human oversight.

Supply chain security is another critical consideration in adaptive cyber resilience. Organizations are interconnected with numerous suppliers and third-party vendors, creating potential vulnerabilities. Assessing and monitoring the security practices of these external partners is essential to protect against supply chain attacks.

Training and awareness programs should be ongoing and adapted to the evolving threat landscape. Cybersecurity education should not be a one-time event but a continuous process that keeps employees informed about the latest threats and best practices.

In summary, adaptive cyber resilience strategies recognize that cybersecurity is a dynamic and ever-changing field. They prioritize agility, proactive threat hunting, robust risk management, and a culture of cybersecurity awareness. While cybersecurity frameworks provide a valuable foundation, organizations must go beyond them to create strategies that can adapt to the evolving threat landscape and protect against the relentless tide of cyber threats. Cyber resilience is not a destination but an ongoing journey of improvement and adaptation.

Conclusion

In this comprehensive book bundle, "Defense in Depth: Network Security and Cyber Resilience," we embarked on a journey through the intricate world of network security and cyber resilience, spanning from the fundamentals to expert-level techniques. Across four distinct volumes, we explored the critical aspects of protecting digital assets, combating cyber threats, and building robust defenses.

In "Defense in Depth Demystified," our journey began with a Beginner's Guide to Network Security and Cyber Resilience. We provided a solid foundation for those new to the field, helping them understand the basics, terminology, and key principles of network security. Armed with this knowledge, readers were equipped to navigate the complex realm of cybersecurity.

In "Mastering Defense in Depth," we delved into Advanced Strategies for Network Security and Cyber Resilience. This volume was tailored for those seeking to elevate their expertise, offering insights into sophisticated defense techniques and strategies. Readers explored cutting-edge solutions to protect against evolving threats and enhance their organization's security posture.

"From Novice to Ninja" was our third volume, serving as a Comprehensive Guide to Defense in Depth in Network Security. It provided readers with an extensive toolkit of skills and practices, allowing them to take a comprehensive approach to network security. With a deep understanding of network architecture, advanced threat intelligence, and access control, they were well-prepared to face the challenges of the digital landscape.

Our final volume, "Defense in Depth Mastery," unlocked Expert-Level Techniques for Unparalleled Cyber Resilience in

Network Security. This volume was designed for seasoned professionals looking to hone their skills and tackle the most sophisticated cyber threats. Readers gained access to cutting-edge strategies, incident response methodologies, and a deeper dive into encryption and access control.

Throughout this book bundle, we emphasized the importance of a proactive and layered defense strategy. We highlighted the evolving threat landscape and the need for organizations to adapt continuously. Cybersecurity is not a one-size-fits-all approach, and the journey toward cyber resilience is ongoing.

In summary, "Defense in Depth: Network Security and Cyber Resilience" offered a comprehensive and progressive exploration of the field. Whether you are a beginner looking to build a solid foundation or an expert seeking to refine your techniques, this bundle has equipped you with the knowledge and skills needed to navigate the complex and ever-changing world of network security and cyber resilience. As you move forward, remember that cyber threats will continue to evolve, and your commitment to ongoing learning and adaptation will be the key to success in safeguarding your digital assets.